THAT
YANKEE
CAT

For Deb and for Hank, without whom,
in their own ways, this book
would never have been completed
and
For the Major and Miss Sassy K. Boodle,
because we loved them.

THAT YANKEE CAT

THE MAINE COON

THIRD EDITION

MARILIS HORNIDGE

Camden, Maine

Down East Books

An imprint of Globe Pequot, the trade division of
The Rowman & Littlefield Publishing Group, Inc.
4501 Forbes Blvd., Ste. 200
Lanham, MD 20706
www.rowman.com

Distributed by NATIONAL BOOK NETWORK

Library of Congress Catalog Card Number 90-72055

ISBN 9781684751235 (paperback)
ISBN 9781684751242 (electronic)

∞™ The paper used in this publication meets the minimum requirements
of American National Standard for Information Sciences—Permanence of
Paper for Printed Library Materials, ANSI/NISO Z39.48-1992.

Contents

Foreword   i

Introduction   iii

1   Whence Came the Cat?   1

2   Who Helped the Cat?   11

3   Here Is the Cat   23

4   Whither Goeth the Cat?   45

5   Tales of the Cat   61

6   On Peaceful Coexistence   77

7   The Home Paramedic and the Impatient Patient   92

Epilogue   101

Appendix   102

Photo insert appears between pages 22 and 23

Foreword

To more people than I can possibly include, I owe my thanks.

First and foremost in the initial stages of this book to Deb Hunter of Wiscasset, Maine, who innocently answered an ad in a local paper asking for information on Maine Coon cats and was pounced upon by an author in search of a path. To the late and much loved Bette Ljostad and her dedicated husband Rod, whose incredible and impressively organized files were my Library of Coon Cat Congress. To longtime breeder Liz Eastman of Bailey's Island, Maine, and to Beth Hicks of Memphis, Tennessee, then editor of *The Scratch Sheet*, now MCBFA's archivist, who constantly and conscientiously kept me on my toes and up-to-date. To the various editors of *The Scratch Sheet*, especially current editor Kit Mounger, presiding genius of the incredible Cat Quilt as well, and to their many correspondents and columnists over the last exciting two decades, who have fought to keep everyone in the Coon Cat World advised of the problems and joys inherent in the breed's rise to Superstar Status—currently the second most popular breed in the U.S. show ring.

To the many Maine Coon breeders and owners from all over the country and abroad who, on the announcement that I was considering an encore update, bravely entrusted to the mail irreplaceable photographs, clippings, and data about the cats they so obviously love—along with encouraging words for the author. To all those involved in and cheering for the first edition, its paperback reincarnation, and the revised edition that followed. To so many Coon cat devotees that I'd be saying "thank you" into infinity—but especially to the indomitable and unstoppable Janet Falconer.

To people from the early days of the Central Maine Cat Club such as Ethelyn Whittemore, the late Alta Smith-Berry, and Vida Grant, who generously shared with me their time, their memories, and their scrapbooks at a time when no one recognized Those Cats as the stars they would become.

To Logan Johnston the implacable, who believed, when no other publisher did, that this was a book with a wide audience, and who has, regrettably, been known to refer to the second edition as *Son of That Yankee Cat* and this one as my *Magnum O-Puss*.

To all the storytellers who wanted to remain anonymous and whom I can thank in no other way.

To the readers of my article on the Maine Coon cat in *Yankee* magazine of December 1976, who were still writing to me long after saying, "Please tell me more." To all the readers, breeders, and fanciers alike, who have written to me over the twenty years after the appearance of the first edition saying, "Please, will you explain. . . ?"

I sincerely hope that I have.

Introduction

"What is a Maine Coon cat?" The lady who asked me was quite serious. No one pays money at the door to go to a cat show who isn't pretty seriously interested in cats.

"It is a distinctive American breed of cat," I said, "that has only recently been reestablished and recognized by all registering and show associations in this country. It is the oldest show breed in North America, and, some people say, the only truly native American breed."

She looked confused. "Maine Coon cats have long, smooth, but shaggy fur," I went on. "They have straight noses, unlike Persians to which everyone compares them; sturdy, strong bodies; and an intelligent, gregarious nature." I showed her several examples of different colors, pointing out other physical characteristics such as the tufted ears and the concentration of fur in the head-to-neck area, making an elegant ruff, and in the hind quarters, forming "britches" that look like a cowboy's chaps. We admired the Coon's distinctive plumy tail.

"But what *is* a Maine Coon cat?" she asked me again. She wasn't asking idly or just being persistently obtuse, I could feel that. She was puzzled.

"There are dozens of legends about them," I tried

again. "We won't even discuss that absurdity about the raccoon crossbreed. Some people think they are a cross between a native wildcat and a domestic cat. Many claim that Maine sea captains brought back Angoras and Persians, which mixed with the local talent. There are those who believe that the original ancestors came over with the Vikings. Every theory has its partisans, and they all have some backing for their theories, however, nobody has proof positive."

"Thank you very much," she said, but as I watched her walk away, I knew that somewhere in her head she was saying to herself, "but really, what is a Maine Coon cat?"

As anyone involved with this old/new breed can tell you, of the ten most asked questions, the first five questions will be variations on the theme—"Just what is a Maine Coon cat?" Next come "How can I tell if the cat I found in Maine is a Maine Coon? How can I get him registered? Is it a legitimate show breed? If it was once recognized as a breed, why did it have to be done all over again? Why are so many conflicting things written about them?"

And at the United Maine Coon Cat Show on October 20, 2001, seated at an information-laden table, surrounded by experts, I heard the same question again. This time it was a serious lady from New Hampshire—gazing admiringly at a handsome redcoated Coon cat behind us in his star dressing room, resting on his considerable laurels and awaiting a return to stage center. "But what makes THAT cat a Maine Coon cat?" she said. Those were her exact words.

Déjà vu all over again.

It is for my earnest questioners, and for the many others who have written and asked me these same questions, that this updated book is written. I hope that it will absorb, answer, and amuse them.

For, to anyone who has ever met one and to everyone who has ever lived with one, the Maine Coon is a very special breed of cat.

1

Whence Came the Cat?

Around the origins of the Maine Coon cat swirls a fog of legend and conjecture as obscuring as the fogs of its homeland. There is a wealth of romantic tradition, of genetic theory, of natural-selection stories so broad and colorful as to be the envy of any other breed. There are dashing sea captains, Mendelian theorists and cracker-barrel P. T. Barnums. None of these tales, be they scrubbed theory or embellished legend, can be proven so conclusively as to eliminate the others. Each has its partisan backers willing to take up the verbal cudgels in defense of their pet theory.

To quote Darwin on the subject, "We know hardly anything about the origin or history of any of our domestic breeds. But, in fact, a breed, like a dialect of a language, can hardly be said to have a distinct origin." He goes even further, "They [the newly developed domestic breed of an animal] will as yet hardly have a distinct name and from being only slightly valued, their history will have been disregarded. When further improved, they will spread more widely and will be recognised as something distinct and valuable and will then probably first receive a provincial name." Although Darwin was talking about breeds of farm animals and birds, if transposed to our day, he

This copy of an old print of Tibetan wild cats in the snow shows many points similar to those of Maine Coons and suggests how the legend that they were originally wild cats tamed by man might have begun. (Photo: Les Hoffman)

could be talking specifically about the Maine Coon cat, whose origin has indeed been disregarded and obscured.

Of the many legendary tales of the Coon cat's beginnings, the one most completely discredited is the best known, the mating of the raccoon and the domestic housecat. This is, of course, a physical impossibility since it is a mating between different species. It is amazing that to this day, this myth crops up among those who would classify the mating between a horse and a cow as a fairy tale. Even a book as recently published as 1974, G. Grilke's *The Cat and Man*, makes use of the idea. Mr. Grilke states, "In the Northeast, it is thought to have been bred from a raccoon because the cat's front claws are divided like a raccoon's." They aren't; and it isn't.

Through the years, the tale's plausibility has been fed by the sight of the cat, since many people think of the tabby-patterned Maine Coon with its ringed tail as the prototype, not realizing that the breed covers the spectrum of cat colors. There are also those who claim that long-ago settlers, seeing the husky form with its large tail prowling the dark, confused the cat with or thought it a relation of the raccoon. This statement has been laid at the door of the Monhegan Islanders, which should cause chuckles or a mild muttering amongst the inhabitants of this best known of the Maine out-islands.

A final touch to this conclusive (I hope) discrediting of the theory is the perfectly matter-of-fact account out of the 1937 edition of the Federal Writer's Project's *Maine: A Guide Down East*. The recorder relates from a "local source" that the breed originated when "a cat from China, Maine" mated with a raccoon. It is only too easy to imagine the scene and the actors in this mini-drama: the fresh-faced, intense, young recorder; the slow-spoken, serious Mainer with his tongue firmly inserted in his cheek. It barely misses being a cliché and ranks as one of the better Coon cat tales for the unwary.

So much for the legendary and impossible raccoon ancestor, although I have no hope that he is well and truly laid to rest. His image forever plays the ghost of the King to the Coon cat's Prince Hamlet.

Next in order of biologically based theories comes the bobcat/housecat cross. This theory, much denigrated at one time, has a great deal to recommend it and many devoted adherents. While it is not a frequent occurrence, the mating of bobcats (which I use as a general term to cover bobcats, lynx, and small wildcats) and domestic cats has been documented and authenticated by authorities as recently as Sanderson's *Living Mammals of the World*, published in 1970. There are eyewitness accounts of matings producing offspring in Texas in 1949 and in North Dakota in 1954 and articles in national magazines about the resultant offspring. The kittens are described in all cases as sturdy, heavily furred specimens with large tufted ears and equally outsized furry feet. Many of the physical characteristics of the bobcat are those distinguishing the Maine Coon, even as a kitten.

Just as the wolf/dog cross is not considered improbable or undesirable, neither is the bobcat/housecat cross. In addition, the bobcat is more prevalent in the northeastern United States even today than is commonly realized, living on the forested necks of land that also support a population of deer, foxes, fishers, and scattered settlements of people. The bobcat population must have been even more dense in earlier times when the Maine Coon's genetic pattern was set.

Now we come to the most romantic and embellished of the origin legends, the tale of Captain Samuel Clough of Wiscasset, Maine, Marie Antoinette, Queen of France, and the royal cats. Its beginning and its end are immutably grounded in fact. As the French Revolution drove to its bloody climax, many plots sprang up to save the royal family. Involved in one such effort toward the latter days was a sea captain named Samuel Clough, who was to bring the queen to the United States in his ship, the *Sally*. All the plots failed. After this documented beginning, tellers of the tale split into two camps.

The romantics say that the captain saw the queen as the classic maiden-in-distress and himself as a seaborne St. George. Certainly he put himself and his crew in grave jeopardy, smuggling on board all sorts of royal household items that would make his mission obvious to any potential informer. It must have cost him or his backers enormous sums in bribery, and the danger from the revolution's spy network must have been considerable. In addition, he seems to have put his own happy home life on the line, for, according to this version, the queen was to come home to live with him and his family. He wrote to his wife (the letters still exist) suggesting improvements and changes in their house and way of living so that the queen might feel more at home. Either he was very sure of his wife's sympathetic nature or he was looking at the entire episode through rose-colored glasses to have imagined Marie Antoinette settled in Maine. This is

to say nothing of the inconvenience to his wife of having a queen, ex-
or not, as a permanent houseguest.

The realists dismiss this entire story as flutter-headed frippery.
Samuel Clough was a New England sea captain, they say, and therefore practical, hardheaded, and adventurous only if well paid. In addition, they state, somewhat pompously, a real Maine Yankee would
never have been emotionally stirred by the Royalist cause so soon after the American Revolution. The realists overlook the fact that by
1793, many people in Maine were wondering if they hadn't just ex-
changed King George for King Congress, and they were exceedingly
suspicious of crowds screaming that they were doing terrible things
only for the good of the people. Underneath the practical exterior of
the Mainer runs a wide streak of the romantic, and it frequently surfaces in the cause of the individual put upon by the State. The realists, ignoring this, contend that the captain was well paid and that
he took off with the cargo after he had faced the possibilities of not
getting the rest of his money and being held in port and possibly
executed.

Whatever the truth of the matter, when the captain sailed, he had
on board furniture, cloth, wallpaper, household china and silver, various ornamental knick-knacks, and (at last they appear) six of the
queen's long-haired cats. Although the French queen has never been
documented as having owned Persian or Angora cats, her penchant
for small, fluffy, cuddly animals is well known. Everything arrived
safely in America. At first the furnishings were carefully stored away,
which would seem to put a crimp in the theory of the avaricious captain. Gradually, however, as the bloody news came in and it became
obvious that no one would be left to claim them, things began to dis-
perse through the house and to the family. And the cats went visiting, as cats do, to become the fur-cloaked, royal ancestors of the
Maine Coon cat.

From Captain Clough we pass on to a much more obscure fellow, a
captain who is mentioned with extreme brevity in all discussions of
possible Coon cat origins and then dropped immediately. Captain
Coon, which is his improbable name, is a tough man to document.
He has even, in one recent newspaper article, been represented as
having been Chinese, a statement sweeping in its inaccuracy and a
non sequitur of the first order. It is tempting to think that someone

5

The Norweign Skogkatt (or Forest Cat), of which Njavos Sangueetah of Zazzara is a glorious example, is certainly more than kissin' kin to the Maine Coon. (Photo: Alice Su)

such as the "local source" in the story of the cat from China, Maine, made up the good captain out of whole cloth and presented him to the gullible public.

Not so. The Captain Coon story is a local legend from the area of Biddeford Pool, Maine. It is one of those stories passed down through oral tradition among people who enjoy stories about their past but who have rarely figured in history books or been prominent on the national political or social scene and have thus been overlooked by mainstream writers. Captain Coon was an English sea captain who owned and operated a trading vessel in the early days of the colonies, and he was exceedingly fond of cats. He traded all up and down the New England coast, and whenever he went on land to do business, his feline army went with him. Predominant in the group, or standing out to the native's eyes because they were unusual, were his longhairs—the Persians and Angoras that were popular in England. Naturally, when the captain fraternized ashore, so did his cats, and when long-haired kittens began appearing in local litters, the amused (or not) owners' comment was, "one of Coon's cats." Being something a little different, these felines began to be encouraged to breed to one another until at last there was indeed a Maine Coon's cat. Or so it goes.

Delving far back into American history, one comes upon the Vikings, and with the Vikings may have come another potential ancestor for the Maine Coon, one known today in the European cat fancy as the Norweign Skogkatt. A judge at a Berlin cat show in 1975, one who was qualified to judge Skogkatts, unofficially stated that in her opinion Maine Coons, several of which appeared in the show, and Skogkatts appeared to be the same breed. There have been many letters between Scandinavian breeders and owners and their opposite numbers in the various Maine Coon organizations remarking on similarities between the two. In 1971, the oldest cat club in Denmark, the Dansk Racekatte Klub, began the practice of donating gold and silver medals to be awarded to Maine Coons.

The Norweign Skogkatt and its Danish and Swedish counterparts, the Racekatte and the Rugkatt, have many physical traits in common with the Maine Coon. They have evolved from a similar rough-terrain, harsh-climate background and have both undergone periods of living wild. The Scandinavian breeds are excellent hunters, and it is not inconceivable that the practical Vikings might have taken some along to their settlements in Greenland and Vineland to keep down the rodent population in grain and food stores.

There is also a possible connection between these Scandinavian charmers and the story of Marie Antoinette and Captain Clough. One of the most ardent Royalists in the French court was the Swedish diplomat Count Axel von Fersen, a gentleman devoted to the monarchy and, tradition says, particularly to the queen. Knowing her love of furry pets and having access to the distinctive cats of his native land, he would seem a logical person to have presented the queen with several kittens, which, by their coloring and markings, would be much more memorable than the popular Persians and Angoras. The reasoning is impeccable even if the proof is nonexistent.

Next in order of the potential European ancestors is the long-haired Russian cat, which was once quite popular on the European continent and which migrated from there to the British Isles, where the cat fancy began and where the unusual is king. In addition, there was once a breed from the Pyrenees called the French Domestic, which is supposed to have been a dead ringer for the Maine Coon. The early French explorers are thought to have brought these cats over to trade with the Indians as destroyers of rodents since there were no domestic felines on the American continent. This would explain the occurrence of Maine Coon types in the southern and southeastern seacoast areas. Neither of these exists as a breed today. There is, however, a small, long-haired cat called the Russian Steppes cat, which many breeders say bears a striking resemblance to the Maine Coon. Since breeders are notoriously loathe to admit that there is any cat that looks like their cat, this carries some weight. So much for the possibilities in the European family tree.

The most probable, although certainly the least picturesque, is what might be called the Darwinian-genesis or you-don't-fool-Mother-Nature theory. Each of the preceding theories could be procrusteanized into this overwhelmingly broad thesis, which is just what makes it suspect to many. Besides, it is much more delightful to think that Marie Antoinette rode to the guillotine reassured that her cats would have a good home, or to picture Leif Erikson with a furry kitten perched on his shoulder or even to imagine the raw-sex wilderness encounter of the domestic puss with the noble savage.

The theory of survival of the fittest by natural selection is plain old general science and makes a lot of sense but no emotional ripples. It goes so: the Maine Coon is the result of nature working on a wide genetic pool on the North American continent with little or no interference from the heavy hand of man. During the entire period of colonization, ships came to the northeastern coast of America with cargoes and crews from all over the world, and with them, their cats. Cats are a seaman's friend, and there were almost always cats aboard trading vessels. Like their human friends, they enjoyed going ashore and striking up acquaintanceships. There would have been on these ships cats of all the basic types that judges and breeders consider the genetic basis for each of today's show breeds, since the ships touched in at ports on all continents. Whether or not a bobcat or a Viking transplant might have entered in here is a moot point; upholders of this theory deem it possible but not necessary. It was a combination of these various cats on the ships plus the harsh climate and terrain, the thinking goes, that eventually resulted in a breed that could be domesticated and also made suitable to its environment by good old natural selection. This solution has a great deal to recommend it. Nature abhors a vacuum (i.e., the lack of domestic felines), but she adores a compromise.

What it all adds up to is that the Maine Coon is a natural breed of cat, or at least the original ones were. After nature, however, comes man. Nature selects traits, if the Darwinian theory holds true at all, that are necessary for survival; man selects traits he finds appealing for reasons aesthetic or practical. Chapter 2 takes up nature's end product and man's progress with it; Chapter 3 gives us man's end product.

At this point, however, to each his own theory of how the cat got there, fact or fancy. The only ones who know for sure are the Maine Coon and the Great Pattern Maker in the Sky.

And they aren't telling.

From the period of the Central Maine Cat Club, Cappy, the 1955 Maine State Champion Coon Cat, shows the sort of form and face that would probably rate prizes today. (Photo: Vida Grant)

2

Who Helped the Cat?

After nature finished combining the genetic ingredients so as to come out with the form and substance of the Maine Coon, man looked upon it and said, "That is some pretty good cat." At least in the state of Maine, he did, and preferring the home-grown product as the traditional Yankee does, that is the core reason for the survival of the Maine Coon as a recognized breed today. The intensely practical Mainer frequently has a great liking for cats. Perhaps this liking stems from an appreciation of cats' capabilities since they were necessary to ship's captain and farmer alike in keeping down the rodent population. Admiration for the attractive packaging of such an efficient worker may also figure in. Whatever the reason, the cats of Maine are likely to be indulged far more than their canine counterparts—particularly if the cat is pretty, spunky, and quirky, all characteristics admired by the Yankee and found in the Maine Coon cat.

The first Maine Coon personality to come down to us through historical record is a black-and-white charmer who answered (occasionally) to the euphonious name of Captain Jenks of the Horse Marines, after a famous music-hall song of the mid-1800's. He belonged jointly to Mrs. F. R. Pierce and her younger brother and was referred to as a Maine cat, which was the breed designation at the time. In a chapter she wrote for Frances Simpson's *The Book of the Cat* (the first comprehensive work on pedigreed and pure-bred cats, published in 1903), Mrs. Pierce says that from her earliest recollection her family had "one to several of the long-haired cats of that variety often called Maine cats." She dates Captain Jenks's command of the household as 1861. Hers is one of the few lengthy documents surviving on the early history of domestic cats in the United States and on the Maine Coon in particular. She not only gives names and dates of cat shows along the eastern seaboard but also names the cats that won them and indulges in occasional side comments on the growing cat fancy itself. She tartly takes to task those who write of the first cat show ever held in the U.S. as being the Madison Square Garden show of 1895. She states emphatically that large shows were held in all the populous eastern cities, although not on a yearly basis, and even as far west as Chicago in the 1870's.

Before these large, organized feline happenings, however, the Maine Coon had begun its long day in the sun, with an eclipse in the middle, as America's native longhair, the oldest established breed in the country, the all-American cat. Every article that mentions Maine Coons in any historical depth states unequivocally that they were shown long before cat shows were popular here or abroad. The date given is usually around the 1860's, and the statement frequently alludes to the state fairs of New England, particularly those of Maine. This is never documented but merely presented as fact.

Now the state fairs of New England had always had livestock shows and competitions as part of their offerings. These were, indeed, one of the fairs' primary reasons for existing. The legendary beginning of the agricultural fair was Elkanah Watson's exhibition of two Merino sheep in the public square in Pittsfield, Massachusetts, in 1807. The townsfolk came to look at the sheep, discuss their good points, and socialize. One imagines that the next year Mr. Watson's sheep, or their progeny, were joined by those of other farmers who considered their livestock just as good. Someone was designated to judge, and so it must have begun.

The holding of livestock shows and fairs became general in New England about 1832. As the scope broadened, exhibits and contests proliferated. By the 1860's farmers had livestock competitions, pull-

ing contests, horse races, and exhibits of newfangled equipment—
some commercial, some home inventions. For the farm wife there
were competitions in baking and handwork of all sorts and in her special areas of farming such as poultry and dairy products. The theory
seems to be that there were also gradually included classes of competi-
tion for household pets. These might have included the precursors of
field and obedience trials for dogs, but for the family feline, they
would have been beauty contests. Temporarily going along with this
train of thought, the Maine Coon (then known as a "coon," a "shag,"
or a "snughead," the derivation of the latter having been irretrievably
lost) was prized as a top-notch house-mouser and barn cat; but it was
also, when forcibly curried into neatness, a regal, handsome, and impressively large figure of a cat. This was, after all, the Victorian era,
which would never have admired Twiggy or the svelte show Siamese.
Thus, supposedly, the Maine Coon became a showcat, a standout
among its short-coated brethren and a class unto itself.

Unfortunately, like so many of the colorful stories surrounding the
Maine Coon, this one sorely lacks corroborative evidence. Nowhere
in the annals of the Maine state fairs of the era, in the meticulous listing of prizes, premiums, and diplomas, or in the recorded events of the
county agricultural societies, is there any mention of domestic pets
being shown. There remain only the small, local, and town exhibits
that were held on a yearly basis but for which there are no records.
Certainly there must have been shows of some variety since in the
large urban shows of the 1870's the Maine Coon is accepted as a definite breed, which implies some sort of standard, however loose it
might be considered today. The arguments and discussions can therefore only concern translation from the standards and rules of one time
to those of another, gradually becoming more stringent. The fact re-
mains that by the time there was an event called a cat show, there
was an accepted breed called the Maine or the Maine Coon cat.

An example of those early big-city shows was the National Cat
Show, a six-day show that began in Boston's Music Hall on January
21, 1878. Listed in the program, a copy of which is preserved in the
Boston Public Library, are twelve Maine Coon cats, one from as far
away as Togus Farm, Maine. They are set apart, competing against
each other only, which is as good evidence as it is possible to get that
they were at that time considered a breed. Shows like this once

Heidi-ho's Heathcliffe II, whose coat, conformation, and cool are equally impressive, shows the male Coon cat's blockier look. Note the variations in length of fur, a Maine Coon characteristic. (Photo: Alice Su)

Majesticats' Classic Delight has a gorgeous and typical Maine Coon coat with outstanding classic tabby markings and a wraparound tail. (Photo: Mark McCullough)

served to keep the Maine Coon in the public eye—a mixed blessing, for in the urban areas, interest in cats and their breeding was growing fast. Out of this interest was to come the cat fancy (a generic term borrowed from the British covering all cat fanciers), show and breeding organizations, and the temporary oblivion of the Maine coon cat.

There was, at this same time, a group of cats known as "coon cats" and not just in the United States, either. Harrison Weir, founder of the English Cat Fancy and author of the "standard of excellence and beauty" which was its core, devoted three chunky paragraphs to them in his preface to *Our Cats: The New Edition* (March 12, 1892). He attributes the "facts" he presents to letters from American cat devotees—a full reproduction is printed in the Maine Coon Breeders and Fanciers' *Scratch Sheet* for fall 2001 (that gem of a newsletter and repository of information both historic and current). Although there are some real howlers included—such as the "fact" that they come "from the islands off the Maine Coast" and that there are cats of a "rich mahogany colour with brushes like a fox," the description adds up in many of its basic parts to the show cat of today.

In May of 1895, when the most famous and largest of the early shows was held at Madison Square Garden in New York, this was all in the future. The show was won hands-down, first place, and best of show, by a brown tabby female Maine cat named Cosie. It must have been a spectacular show, numbering 176 animals in all and including two ocelots, two "wildcats," and three civet cats. The number of Maine cats is not easily ascertained since they were classified along with Persians and Angoras as "longhairs." All cats were categorized first by hair length and then by sex. Today's organizations would be horrified by the loose standards, classifications of "he-cats" and "she-cats" disregarding neutering, and prizes for categories like "homeliest" and "heaviest." An orchestra played night and day and a lady cat trainer gave exhibitions of her "Wonderful Trained Cats" every afternoon and evening of the show. Patterned after London's Crystal Palace Show of 1871, it was a great success, financially and as a public relations showcase for the various breeds. At least it was as far as the people were concerned. No one ever asked the cats, all of which would have

16

Her beautifully varied coat, Elizabethan ruff, and elegant white gloves make Timberwind's Purr Fect Willow the epitome of the feminine Maine Coon.
(Photo: Carolee Brakewood)

probably voted no, since the show was held during an unseasonable heat wave.

The New York Show, however, did not immediately develop into the annual prestigious event it was later to become; the Boston show circuit did. One of Mrs. Pierce's handsomest brown tabby Maine cats, King Max, dominated this classic for three years, winning in 1897, '98, and '99, until defeated by his son in 1900. At the opening of the twentieth century, "show fever" hit the fancy, and cat shows began to spread from the Northeast to the Midwest and finally to the West Coast. These were reported in magazines of wide circulation, devoted solely to such occurrences, called *Cat Journal* and *Cat Review*, copies of which are collector's items today.

At about the same time, the Cat Fanciers Association (CFA), founded in 1908 and second oldest of the current registry and judging associations in North America, was keeping the only breed record books we have of this period. This was the CFA Stud Book and Registry. In Book I, twenty-eight Maine cats, as they were still known, were listed under a special proviso that depended on a sworn statement that the sire and dam were "same breed, long hair and that neither is a short-hair." It is interesting to note that CFA Reg. #5 is a tortoiseshell female Maine cat named Molly Bond.

After such an auspicious beginning, snobbery began to raise its ugly head. As cats and their breeding began to attract more and more interest countrywide, the improved breeds became status symbols. Dorothy Champion, who wrote several books on the early days of cats and the fancy, recounts watching a judging in the early 1900s. In this judging, a Maine cat that she considered a much better specimen than the winner came in second in the long-haired class. The judge freely admitted giving the blue ribbon as she did simply because the winning cat had recently been imported from England. It was an indication of what was coming.

Slowly the Maine Coon began disappearing from the ranks of registry and show. In Portland, Oregon, in 1911, in a show of 170 entries, the Maine Coon had its last big recorded victory for over forty years when a "long-haired blue Maine cat" took first place in his class and best of show. After that, Maine Coons slipped slowly into the background and were shown only occasionally under

AOV, the fancy's Any Other Variety or miscellaneous category.

During the next forty years, the Maine Coon as a breed was taken seriously only Down East, by natives and their summer visitors. Many Maine families continued to take pride in their cats, and even kept track of their lineage. Mrs. Ethelyn Wittemore of Augusta, Maine, has been called the godmother of the Maine Coon cat. Like Mrs. Pierce before her, Mrs. Wittemore's family had Maine Coons for as long as she could remember. She kept, at one time, handwritten longstanding records of their parentage and progeny and must hold the record for the tallest Coon cat family tree with recorded roots, the first family of Coon-catdom. She was a prototype of the dedicated amateur breeder whose devoted interest and determined effort kept the breed image alive over the years when little attention was paid to it elsewhere. Most breeders and owners, however, kept few written records, and without some fresh impetus toward this as a policy, the breed might have been lost.

In 1953 the next part of the framework for success came along. The Central Maine Cat Club (CMCC), which was to put an end to the Maine Coon's slide into a mere regional oddity, gave both the impetus toward recordkeeping and a showcase for the breed. The brainchild of Alta Smith and Ruby Dyer, two young professional women in Skowhegan, Maine, the club was intended to provide attention for all cats in the form of publicity and shows, a service they felt was much needed. Some pedigreed cats were shown and judged, but the emphasis was on the others. Of these, of course, the Maine Coon was the hometown hero and for the first time in many years was publicly recognized as a distinct breed. This necessitated a written description for the judges of the appearance and fine points of the Maine Coon cat. In addition, birth records were sold by the club, the first time this had ever been done outside of organized registering bodies like CFA. These were to be the written records from which later generations of Maine Coons were to trace their ancestry, relying totally on the judgment, accuracy, and veracity of the owner and breeder.

The Central Maine Cat Club was, perhaps, a regional maverick, but for just that reason it attracted many cat lovers who were turned off by the rarefied atmosphere of the world of the big organizations with their rigid formats and requirements. The first CMCC show was held on June 21, 1953. It combined the cat show itself with an exhibition of photographs of cats and was held in a small barn-theater outside Skowhegan. To the amazement of the founders, it drew forty feline entries, twenty photographic entries, and more than 200 spectators. Using the same format, the club held shows in which the Coon cat was the featured attraction for the next ten years. Usually considered a great human interest story, the year's Maine State Champion Coon Cat frequently turned up in newspaper pictures in places like Kansas City, Tampa, Austin, or San Francisco. Thus, the name, and often the image—for Maine Coons are extremely photogenic—were kept alive in the public mind.

In the meantime, the CMCC shows outgrew the barn, the elementary school gym, the high school gym, and every other large local meeting place. By the fifth show, there were more than a hundred cats entered, and the club included members from thirty-eight states and fifteen foreign countries. The eleventh and final show was held in the Augusta Armory. By 1963, however, the organization began to be too unwieldy to continue as strictly amateur. It was obviously fish or cut bait—become a large organized body or stop. Miss Smith, who had become Mrs. Berry but was still the mainspring of the club, opted for stopping. There was no one to take her place, and the Central Maine Cat Club ceased to be.

By that time, however, for the Maine Coon cat, the framework was up and the foundation was solid. For the fourth show, in 1965, Dr. Rachael Salisbury, a breeder and judge affiliated with the larger organizations of the fancy and a summer resident of Maine, had drawn up a standard by which Maine Coons could be judged. She had also officiated at early shows and trained local judges. Although the language of this first standard was not as precise as that used today, echoes of the CMCC standard can be discerned in the present one. Breeders and owners had become accustomed to keeping records and felt that it was important. People from outside the area were beginning to be aware that Maine Coon cats existed and that they had credentials. What was especially important was that people in other parts of the country were starting to breed and show Maine Coons as well as keeping them as pets. They were

A recent show photo gives an idea of what cats, owners, and judges face in the ring when attempting to demonstrate conformation, coat, and special points—not to mention cool all around. Specialty Judge Dewane Barnes and JohnsBay Bowdoin give an idea of how it's done. (Photo: Jamie Doherty)

shown under the AOV classification, of course, but they were beginning to be shown again in appreciable numbers.

In August of 1968, six Maine Coon breeders and owners held a meeting in Salisbury, Connecticut. From this gathering was to come the single strongest force in the last stage of the Maine Coon's comeback, the Maine Coon Breeders and Fanciers Association (MCBFA). The group's aim was to unite everyone interested in the future of the Maine Coon cat to work for its re-recognition as a breed by the official organized show circuit. One of the earliest projects was, as one of the original members called it, the "show-in," an effort to place as many Maine Coons as possible in as many shows as possible. The group prepared packets of information to be mailed to anyone requesting them, not an easy job at a time when information on Coon cats was sparse and fragmented. Members put out a quarterly newsletter of some note and literary merit called, aptly enough, *The Scratch Sheet*. And they began work on the hardest, thorniest, and most important item of all, devising a unified standard acceptable to all Maine Coon breeders for adoption by themselves and acceptance by all registering bodies to qualify the Maine Coon for championship status once again.

Five years later, all but one of the registering associations of the North American cat world had accepted the Maine Coon. Over two thousand packages of information had been mailed out to interested parties. Articles were appearing in newspapers and magazines in North America and in France, England, Germany, and the Scandinavian countries. Once again the Maine Coon was being mentioned in books on breeds, although not always with notable accuracy. There were MCBFA members in thirty-four states, four provinces, and six foreign countries. The Maine Coon cat was on the comeback trail.

By 1976 the All-American cat had come home. The Cat Fanciers Association, ironically the last holdout, finally granted championship status to one of its original breeds. The Maine Coon could once more be shown with its peers in all cat shows. No more AOV, no more second-class citizenship. Breed councils within the organizations began to take over part of the work from MCBFA, which retained its status as an unaffiliated group dedicated to the breed. MCBFA itself had grown so large as to necessitate dividing into regional sections and redrafting its constitution.

Any show-bred animal goes through this process, but it is perhaps more visible in the case of the Maine Coon cat because of its unique now-you-see-him-now-you-don't career. The breed stood at this point at the beginning of a new wave of popularity. The next two chapters will discuss just that: the cat that was and is being formed, and the forces, both the fancy and genetics, that are at work on the breed.

A Maine Coon litter, like this one from City Paws Cattery can be full of most charming surprises.
(Photo: M.P. Cristoforo, Jr.)

His red coat glowing in the sunlight, Dirigo's Swift River Ruffian belies his name...
(Photographer: Beth Kus)

while Glenncourt Chief Tecumseh of Kumskaka at nine months looks stoic and plans to do in his ribbon as soon as the camera goes away. (Photo: Phyllis Tobias)

Tomeran's Jack London sports absolutely outstanding ear tufts. (Photo: David Eckard)

while the prize for most incredible ruff would have to be split between Bentley's King Edward III…
(Photo: Blue Ribbon Photography)

and Chancery's Jonathan, the sort of decision nobody would want to make.
(Photo: Wolcott Studio)

Texas Belle's Jim Dandy, a brown classic tabby with white, certainly lives up to his name with the charm of Ashley Wilkes and the aplomb of Rhett Butler. (Photo: Helmi Flick)

Calicoon's Hooligan, a red mackerel tabby with wonderful whiskers and boon-docker paws, really lets the cat out of the bag. (Photo: Dorothy Holby)

3

Here
Is
the
Cat

A breed of any kind must have a written and defined standard, an ideal to measure up to or to be
judged against, whether the judging is done as strictly
as in a show ring or as casually as in the interested
observer's eye. The development of a reliable but not
restrictive standard, however, is a difficult undertak-
ing. It provides material for meetings lasting into the
small hours, schism in the ranks, and personal ven-
dettas. It is a wonder that a workable standard is ever
achieved without bloodshed.

In order to be effective, a standard must be flexible
but not indefinite, definite but not rigid. An inflex-
ible standard produces exaggerations of desirable
traits into grotesqueries; a too-permissive standard results in an undefined animal. The devising of a standard is a verbal tightrope walk over a shark pool of
critics. Breeders take themselves and their cats very
seriously. They and, ultimately, judges form the animal presented to the world as the prime example of
the breed. The only yardstick is the standard and the
judges' interpretation of that standard with regard to
the particular member of the breed being judged. A
judge looking at a cat in hand is forming his image of
what the cat should look like from words on paper,
written by the breeders' association and accepted by

An all-star lineup of color and pattern, from left to right—Manhatta's Billingsgate (a black smoke kitten of four months) and overseeing adults KittyUp Starbuck of Manhatta (black smoke with white), CloisterCoon SunDance of Manhatta (a classic red tabby), and KittyUp Skrimshander of Manhatta (black smoke).
(Photo: Marilyn Lehrfield)

Ktaadin's Chelsea captures the ladylike air of many Maine Coons . . .
(Photo: G. Malesky)

. . . while Hilltop Park Paloma of Hampton Coon epitomizes the feral look as an alternative—with Olympic gymnast agility and right-at-you stare . . . (Photo: David Lamberton)

. . . and Nascat Finn McCool's gaze is enough to give one pause (to make the inevitable Maine Coon pun).
(Photo: Helmi Flick)

the organization that the judge represents. This may sound simplistic, but it is a concept not quickly apparent to the spectator. There is a great deal of room for personal interpretation, which winds up with breeders clamoring that they have been misunderstood and judges begging for clarity and precision.

A breed standard covers the total physical appearance of the cat: size and often shape of each part; color and pattern of coat; eyes; "leather," which means nose and paw pads; proportion; and conditioning. Judges' forms often cover over thirty physical traits. For all breeders (and for some popular breeds the numbers run into the thousands) to agree on all these traits and put them into words so that the judge will be able to picture exactly the cat they have in mind is a neat piece of verbal legerdemain.

This concept is monumentally important. No one trait should stand out. All the pieces should blend into a harmonious whole—to misquote Shakespeare, "The elements should be so mixed in him that Nature might stand up and say to all the world, THIS is a cat." Exaggeration of any trait winds up as caricature (let us not name names, but any cat show neophyte can spot the examples). Of all cat breeds, the Maine Coon is probably the most complete package. After all, while not every person agrees on what makes another *person* beautiful, there is usually agreement as to the presence of charm, appeal, and charisma. And the Maine Coon, the genuine article, has it.

After this preamble, after the long years of hard work, here stands the Maine Coon cat. For some reason, the sight of one at a cat show tends to make spectators relaxed, nostalgic, and talkative. It is somewhat similar to the attitude of people who happily tell antique dealers, "My grandmother had one of those."

The Maine Coon of today is inclined to be a large cat, although not the bruiser of legend. Twelve to fifteen pounds is considered a good size for a male, with the females running ten to twelve. The Maine Coon's legendary size has sometimes led to breeding for gigantism, which is unfortunate. Breeding for one trait too often comes at the expense of another, thus losing the overall picture. The cat looks sizeable anyway, because of its distinctive coat and stocky conformation. The fur is long, although it varies in length, rather like a custom-fitted garment, as opposed to the

The straight Maine Coon nose is another of the outstanding characteristics of the breed. Here is Zig-Krn's Coon Son of Enchantment, showing off his charming profile and his outstanding whiskers. (Photo: Jim Caparelli)

*A dauntingly dramatic duo of brown "patched" tabbies are littermates
Gordon and Bailey of Texas Belle . . .* (Photo: Betsy Gaither)

. . . followed by a real triple play starring, from the top down, Nonesuch's Oliver, Timothy, and Erik. All are red mackerel tabbies, one (Erik) plain, the others cameos. (Photo: John Ewing)

31

Persian's bushy all-one-length coat. The fur on the front of the Maine Coon's shoulders is shorter in comparison, although still much longer than that of the shorthaired breeds. It gradually becomes longer as it progresses down the spine, ending in heavy, shaggy fur on the hindquarters, a conformation referred to as britches or chaps. Down the sides and under the stomach, the fur is long and full. The neck is embellished by a ruff, which may indeed look like an Elizabethan ruff going all the way around (although this is rare), or may look like a hood with a ruffle under the chin. In the latter case, the long fur goes smoothly down the back and sides, fluffs out into muttonchop whiskers at the sides, and spills out from under the chin in a ruffled cascade. There are heavy tufts in and on the ears. The feet are also heavily furred, increasing their apparent size until some Maine Coons appear to be stalking about in boon-dockers. There are even tufts on the bottom of their paws. One theory holds that this is the reason for the cats' ability to walk or run lightly and in surefooted style across the snow. In practice, it also leads to iceballs between the toes.

The texture of Maine Coon fur is fine but at the same time thick, like that of a gigantic, long-furred kitten. The coat has a lustrous sheen, a feel somewhat like that of antique satin, and comes in a fashionable array of colors, which will be discussed later.

On the subject of the coat's variations due to season and climate, I would like to quote Connie Condit, longtime breeder and articulate champion, who said it better than I could in an article in *Cat World* magazine. "The coat is also very subject to seasonal change. In warm weather or warm climates, many Maine Coons shed to their 'shorts' with only their tails retaining a long-haired appearance. Contrary to some legends, the Maine Coon does well in all climates, but being a practical Downeaster, he dresses appropriately."

And then there is The Tail. The Maine Coon's tail is his pride and joy. It is plumy and at the same time shaggy. The fur is very long and extremely full. The tail is a banner and is carried as such. To say merely, as the standards do, "long, wide at the base, fur long and flowing," is like a dry, botanical description of an American Beauty rose.

The standard Maine Coon head is one distinctive point separating him from his longhaired cohorts. It can have a feral, half-wild look, given by a nose with the characteristic that the fancy terms "straightness." This straightness is not that seen in the bust of Nefertiti, but is actually a gentle in-curve from the forehead to the point at which the nose leaves the face and straight from there on. There is further a squareness to the muzzle, which is indeed referred to as a muzzle. Most cats have noses, but muzzle is the right word for the Maine Coon's, carrying as it does a connotation of the wild. Here, too, there has been some exaggeration, with the occasional breeder going for long, long noses, a trait referred to by other breeders as "the Aardvark Syndrome." Once again, proportion is the key. The nose must fit the face so that the viewer does not say, "Oh, *there* is a nose" but rather, "My, what a *feline*." Another controversy has grown up over the feral or "wild" look versus the "sweet" or "handsome" face. Both sides have their adherents, beauty being, as ever, in the eye of the beholder.

The ears, being proportionately large and wide at the base contribute to the wild look, as do the outstanding tufts of fur springing from the inside of the ear and seeming to fill it. These tufts are much fuller and longer than those of any other breed. The tufts on the tops and tips of the ears, which are almost vestigial in some and so heavy as to be reminiscent of the lynx and bobcat in others, are a genetic puzzle to breeders and an enchantment to photographers. They add another grace note from the wild and times past to the Maine Coon's appearance.

The eyes may be green, gold, or copper, although white cats may be, in addition, blue-eyed or odd-eyed (eyes of differing colors). White cats of any breed have a genetic makeup that defies description or easy analysis, and they are somehow held unaccountable for any variation from the norm by the indulgent fancy, rather like child prodigies. Large, round, and set at an oblique angle to its nose, the Maine Coon's eyes remind many people of those of an owl.

As for the body of the cat, the silhouette is proportionately rectangular. The chest is full, and, the standards agree, the neck is medium long, rather balancing the long and equally substantial tail. In the mature male, the neck becomes thick and muscular. The legs are of medium length in proportion to body length, resulting in the required rectangular conformation. The paws are large and round with their prominent tufts.

Chancery's Jonathan is a silver mackerel tabby with a stunning ruff and subtle markings . . .
(Photo: Judy and Dale Liggett)

while Bentley's King Edward III, a black smoke, looks both regal and exotic.
(Photo: J. H. Robbins)

Coon is a black-and-white, the gray touches in his fur being due to a bout of illness and reaction to medication. (Photo: Jim Caparelli)

The number of claws in those paws was perhaps the most controversial of all issues in the final stages of setting up a standard.
The traditional Maine Coon was frequently a polydactyl or many-
toed cat, a genetic mutation that occurs with great frequency in
the upper northeastern United States. In the greater Boston area,
for example, almost 12 percent of the feline population shows this
trait, which to some people is endearing but to others is a deformi-
ty. Whatever the reason for its abundance in this geographic area,
the "poly" or snowshoe-footed cat is part of the Maine Coon legend. Polydactylism was so dear to the hearts of the original group
of enthusiasts who drew up the MCBFA standard, that, rather than
divide the ranks, a special classification with its own standard was
set up for cats possessing the trait. This was the last variation on
the standard to fall victim to the striving for a single standard to be
adopted fancy-wide. Some breeders who love "poly" cats still keep
and breed a few as specialty kittens, although they cannot be
shown except under the A.O.V. category. The practice is frowned
on as pure indulgence by colleagues and competitors.

It might be mentioned at this point that the Maine Coon
rarely reaches its full growth and development until the age of
three years. At this point, it is a sturdy, chunky individual with the
body of an athlete in the clothes of Beau Brummel.

The Maine Coon comes in every color, pattern, and combination possible in the feline world; and each breeder, each area,
each owner has a favorite. Only the Persian can equal the variety.
The Coon cat coat, moreover, is such a showy one that the color
and pattern do not seem to disappear into the texture but rather
are enhanced by it. The names given to colors and patterns by
judges are not always easily comprehensible to laymen. Some are
obvious, some have historical background, and some must simply
be accepted by common usage.

First come the solid colors, which seem deceptively simple.
White, of course, is white—a bright, clear white. Cream is the off-
white of untreated fisherman sweaters and must be free of all markings and shadings. This is referred to as "one level shade." Black is
deep and dense with no hint of rust. This is difficult to achieve,
however, because the gene for black is sometimes accompanied by
another that changes it slightly, resulting in a black cat that, if it is

outdoors much of the time, develops a rusty tint. The only solid color Maine Coons do not come in is brown, although tradition says they once did. Blue means gray, blue-gray to be sure, a color once referred to as Maltese. That lovely orange-marmalade shade is called red, provided again that the coat is one level shade. If the red coat color is exceedingly pale, it will be called cream.

However, if a black, blue, or red cat has a white undercoat that shows only when the fur is ruffled up, it is then considered a smoke. If, on the other hand, a white cat has colored tips on the fur of its outer coat, it is classified as a cameo if the tips are red or a smoke if the tips are black.

So much for the simple part. Next come the patterns. First of all, because it is so easily recognizable, is the calico, the "lucky money cat" of Down East fable. This pattern calls for half to two-thirds of the body being white with a patchwork quilt of red and black elsewhere. The desirable proportion of white to color varies from organization to organization. Next there are the parti-colors, which might be roughly translated as white and one other color. It is generally held that to qualify as a parti-color, one-third of the body must be white with the preferred areas consisting of bib, belly, and all four paws. The "other" may be solid red or solid black or solid blue.

The tabby pattern is probably the most universally well known of all cat coats, the backyard tiger of the urban world. It is also the traditional Maine Coon cat suit, the one that gave rise to the coon/cat-cross legend. The reason for its omnipresence is that tabby markings are genetically dominant, a fact many breeders have found to their dismay when breeding for solids. Many cats that look solid in adulthood were born with faint stripes that faded over time. Such animals therefore carry the hidden tiger in their genetic tanks.

As meticulously defined by the standards, tabbies fall into two patterns: the mackerel tabby and the classic tabby. Basically, the mackerel tabby has stripes all over with a connecting line running down its spine (hence, mackerel); and the classic tabby has stripes on its legs, head, and tail, but the rest of it looks, as one breeder aptly puts it, "like a marble cake in the middle." This is also referred to in some cases as a "patched tabby."

Tabbies come in just about every color combination with the stripes and/or pattern being a dark version of the base color. In show, the color class is called by the name of the base coat, as in brown tabby, the classic pattern, or brown mackerel tabby. If, however, the tabbies have the often-seen white feet and neck ruffle, some organizations then consider them to be parti-colors or to require the phrase "with white" to be added to the cat's designation.

Unfortunately, many people think of the Maine Coon cat as coming ONLY in this pattern and color, considering them the "real" Maine Coons. The glorious variety of colors and patterns belies this—all you have to do is see a handsome fellow in a Maine Coon tuxedo (black with white bib and -tucker), or the sun shining on (and out of) a glossy golden "red" Maine Coon coat as its owner sleeps in a window, to be fascinated and charmed by the Maine Coon's infinite variety.

The tortoiseshell cat could well be described as a basic black cat with large and well-defined patches of red and cream. This pattern is frequently accompanied by a blaze, which means that the face is evenly divided between black and one of the other colors, giving a striking harlequin appearance. The tortoiseshell with white has white paws, bib, and belly. Then there is a configuration referred to as torbie, a hybrid word for the combination of tortoiseshell and tabby. A torbie is a tortoiseshell with stripes instead of patches of color. Unfortunately, tortoiseshell is often referred to as tortie, which sounds so like torbie as to confuse the novice.

If, in addition, the word "smoke" is used with any of these color patterns, it means that the cat looks bleached, rather like the patina and shade acquired by old, worn denim. This shade results from the white undercoat mentioned in the discussion of solid colors.

There are also suitable nose and paw pad colors that go with each coat color, rather like matching accessories, although some organizations consider them only as a secondary or desirable trait. In general, white and red have "leather" in shades of pink to brick red, depending on the intensity of coat color; black, blue, and patterns with these colors predominant have leather in shades of black and brown.

Since the Maine Coon is available in such a wide and diverse spectrum, some breeders seem to outdo themselves. One laughingly said that she tried to breed patriotic kittens for the bicentennial year, crossing a red-and-white female with a blue male. Much

Stonehill's Ephraim is a cream tabby with white who looked like this at one year . . .
(Photo: M. Lenz)

and like this several years later, going to prove the old saw about Maine Coons taking some time to mature. (Photo: K. Robinson)

Ktaadin's J. J. shows off her blaze. (Photo: S. Richardson)

to everyone's surprise, except, no doubt, the cat's, she wound up with a blue-and-white with pinkish-cream touches, which was pretty close.

The Maine Coon thus pictured in the reader's mind should be a sturdy, handsome specimen of cathood. The temperament of the cat is tailor-made to fit its looks. It is as delightful and personable to live with as it is to look upon.

In describing temperament and personality, generalities frequently produce stereotypes and as such must be avoided. For the purpose of this book, I surveyed breeders and owners of Maine Coons, and enlisted the aid of Beth Hicks—whose network of breeders, owners, and fanciers verges on the encyclopedic—asking them to describe the charms of their cats. The answers ran in length from a postcard to seventeen pages. One of the more succinct as well as expressive was: "Dignified but not pompous; demonstrative but not gushy; definite but not excessive." Another of my personal favorites was: "SMART, SMART, SMART (but not stuck-up about it)."

Beth's responses from an international brigade were just as glowing. From Australia, "My first one because of beauty . . . my second one and third one and fourth one because I fell in love with the temperament." From New Zealand, "I've never had a cat like this before . . . they make you feel special. . . ." From Sweden, "I wanted a long-haired cat that looked like a *cat*." From the Netherlands, "They are extremely addictive; they should come wrapped in a package with a warning."

Several adjectives ran like a thread through all the responses. The first and by far the most frequent was "intelligent." Right behind it was "affectionate," coupled with "demonstrative." There were phrases like "people-oriented" and "family oriented" and "good company." Many referred to their cats as friends, somewhat telling since most pet owners see themselves in a more parental role. "Sense of humor" and "sense of proportion" appeared, as did "know their own minds" and "decorative (and don't they know it!)."

All this may seem suspiciously anthropomorphic, but a study made at U.C.L.A. in the early 1970s showed that the information-processing parts of the brain develop faster in animals that are handled, talked to, and stroked during the first several months of life. The appealing Maine Coon kitten generally gets this treatment and responds to it with affection and increasing intelligence.

There were many comments on the Maine Coon's predilection for playing in and with water. One breeder had a female who learned to turn on the tap to watch the water, and there were many stories of kittens and full-grown adults who loved to play in their water dishes. Since the original Maine Coons were an outdoor breed, they are fond of the outside world, although they will live contentedly indoors, and they are about the best mousetrap around.

The distinctive vocal style of the Maine Coon came in for a great deal of discussion. The Maine Coon voice has quite a range, and the cats are capable of making many entirely different noises that they use quite obviously as a language. Their version of the traditional "mew" is a very small noise, ludicrous coming from such a strapping animal, but it is used only in social situations, such as a gentle reminder of the approach of dinnertime. After that, each cat seems to develop its own vocabulary, most of which is not susceptible to phonetic renderings. There is a high, trilling churring that means, "Look out, here I come!" Another beeping noise often means, "I can't find it." One of the most raucous purrs in catdome is used in situations ranging from showing affection to saying smugly, "I dood it and I'm glad."

One of the most telling bits of description, however, came from a very articulate breeder who has bred and lived with several other breeds of cat as well as Maine Coons. She says that they have extremely sex-differentiated personalities, a statement borne out by conversations with other breeders and owners. The females are matriarchs-in-the-making, full of charm and affection, with an implacable, quiet determination to have their own way. They are also excellent hunters. The males, on the other hand, are little boys. If they were cast into human form, they would have frogs in their pockets, freckles and dirt on their faces, and complete confidence that the world revolves around them.

So here at last, firmly on large, furry feet, stands the Maine Coon cat, past, present . . . and what about the future? This, of course, depends in large part on the breeders and judges, on genetics, and on an added and sometimes controversial outside factor that the Maine Coon alone of all breeds has. All of this will be discussed in the next chapter.

4

Whither
Goeth
the
Cat?

Finally standing in the show spotlight, the
Maine Coon's future might seem all cream and
chopped liver. The tendency, however, when a
popular product is achieved, is to continue refining
and promoting, not only to sustain but to further the
popularity. In the case of the pedigreed cat, the
forces driving that process are the same ones that
shaped the animal in the first place: genetics and the
show registry organizations of the cat fancy.

Genetics, to take first things first, is an extremely
complex subject—fascinating to many fanciers, a
headache to the average breeder, and of only passing
interest to the general public. It is not an exact
branch of the biological sciences in that all the facts
are not known; new facets are constantly coming to
light, giving rise to new theories to confuse, con-
found, and delight geneticists and to dismay and frus-
trate breeders. As is true of many of the various sciences, genetics has developed a vocabulary of its own.
In the following oversimplification, any unfamiliar
term will be explained as it is used.

At the risk of seeming pedantic and with the off-
hand ease derived from recent intensive study, I shall
begin with genes, as in elementary general science
courses. The gene is a biological unit within the

body's cells that determines inherited physical, and some say mental, characteristcs. Genes occur in colonies called chromosomes, which look like strings of beads and contain many genes. Chromosomes come in pairs, somewhat like twins but not necessarily identical, containing genes governing similar traits. At the time of reproduction, these pairs split up and then join with one of the chromosomes from the other parent, thus forming for the new individual a new pair with traits from each parent. So much for generalities.

The inherited exterior characteristics of the cat are determined by nineteen pairs of chromosomes. The quickest introduction to the simple part of genetics is to show how this works in determining the sex of the kitten. The chromosomes that carry the sex genes are of two types, commonly called X and Y. Female cats are XX per pair, and male cats are XY. The diagram below, which should vividly recall classroom days, is an illustration of this.

		Male Cat	
		X	Y
Female Cat	X	XX	XY
	X	XX	XY

Thus, any resultant XX is a female kitten, and an XY is a male; and the chances of either are fifty percent per kitten, not overall.

From here on, the subject goes from complex to complicated to esoteric. (Books and articles for further study are given in the Appendix.) The gene for basic coat color, which in cats is a choice between black and red, is carried only on the X chromosome. The color genes are termed sex-linked, therefore, and are written, in simplistic form, X^r (red) and X^b (black). The male cat can, since this is true, have only one color as his base, which is the general explanation for the lack of calico males so dear to the hearts of legendmakers. Obviously, a pure black male and a pure black female will produce only pure black kittens; the same goes for red. However, a black female and a red male are a story of a different color. The diagram for this mating would be as follows:

46

Red Male

		X^r	Y
Black Female	X^b	X^bX^r	X^bY
	X^b	X^bX^r	X^bY

The males are black, the females have both black and red, and the amounts and placement within the coat will be determined by other genetic elements within the remainder of the chromosomes.

This brings us to another set of words much used by breeders and geneticists—genotype and phenotype. The actual genetic makeup of the animal is called the genotype; the outward appearance of the animal is called the phenotype. The punchline in cat genetics is, "What you see ain't always what you got."

First of all, there are dominant genes and recessive genes. The dominant genes "cover" the recessive. As an example from the feline family in general, short hair (L) is dominant over long hair (l). When speaking in genetic shorthand, the dominant gene is given a capital letter; the recessive is given the same letter in lower case. Therefore, we know Maine Coons all receive recessive genes for long hair from both parents; otherwise the short-hair gene (L) would cancel out the long-hair gene (l).

The pairing of a dominant gene and a recessive gene is called heterozygous; the pairing of dominants or recessives is called homozygous. The effect of any recessive gene is therefore seen only when it is homozygous. This is vitally important to breeders since many traits in breed standards are recessive.

An example of this is the Maltese gene, which geneticists call D/d (presumably for Dense/dilute), the D representing non-Maltese and d, Maltese. Maltese, you will remember from Chapter 3, means gray, which the fancy calls blue. The Maltese (d) or recessive gene modifies the basic coat color. When it is present in homozygous form, black becomes gray, red becomes cream. The non-Maltese dominant (D) simply deepens existing colors. Therefore, the recessive gene will not show up in the phenotype, although it may be present in the genotype. Here, followed through two matings, is an example of this. A red male is bred to a cream female.

Red Male

	X^r - D	Y - D
Cream Female X^r - d	X^r/X^r - D/d	X^r/Y - D/d
X^r - d	X^r/X^r - D/d	X^r/Y - D/d

Thus, all the kittens, male and female will look red but will carry the recessive dilute gene. Now a mating between one of these males and a cream female gives quite a different litter.

Red Male from Litter 1

	X^r - d	Y - D
Cream Female X^r - d	X^r/X^r - d/d	X^r/Y - D/d
X^r - d	X^r/X^r - d/d	X^r/Y - D/d

The litter would then consist of two red kittens carrying the dilute gene and two cream kittens. In deference to the geneticists who will by now be screaming foul, I must aver that since the D/d gene is not sex-linked, it is not necessary to have a red male or a cream female. It could just as easily be the other way around, my diagramming being simplified in order to present the point with as few sidesteps as possible.

Volumes have been and are being written on the subject of genetics, which is of such vital importance to the breeder. Some breeders dive happily into such study, having the puzzle turn of mind; to others it is a somewhat dry necessity. Still others prefer to be surprised and constantly are. The breeder uses knowledge of the cat's background from its pedigree, which lists color and pattern of its ancestors, plus his or her own knowledge of genetics. Colors and patterns fall in and out of vogue in varying parts of the country. Some breeders on their own initiative specialize in certain colors or patterns. The breeder's need for knowledge of genetics leads to an equally important need for lasting, accurate, and complete pedigree records. These records are kept by the organizations of the fancy.

To reiterate, the fancy is an overall term for anyone who breeds, shows, owns, or admires cats. The term, as well as much of the organizational impetus and form, is a British import but is now used worldwide. A cat fancier is a person who has an interest in or fancies cats and therefore is a member of the fancy. In order to understand the size and scope of the problem facing Maine Coon adherents in the drive for re-recognition, here is a simplified explanation of the organizations that make up the cat fancy in North America.

Prime among the problems is the fact that there are many organizations, not one governing body as in the dog fancy's American Kennel Club (AKC). Perhaps it is too easy to point out the personality differences between dog lovers and cat lovers to account for such a contrast. At any rate, there are, at the present writing, eight working organizations in the North American cat world. Each has as its reason for existence the registry and showing of cats, specifically pedigreed cats. Many shows also have a provision for the showing of nonpedigreed cats in a division known as Household Pet. Many people have compared the relationship between the cat fancy as a whole and its various organizations to that of the Protestant church in America with its various branches. Irreverent as this may sound, it cuts close to the bone. There have been bitter arguments about interpretation of basic concepts, which have resulted in rifts and separations within and between organizations. There are partnerships without amalgamation but with mutual reciprocity, one organization's registration being accepted to show in events sponsored by another. There is also a basic solidarity between organizations when attacked by outsiders.

The American Cat Association (ACA) is the oldest of the organizations, having been founded in 1904. The Cat Fancier's Association (CFA) is second only in age, having been organized in 1906 as an outgrowth of the ACA. In every other numerical designation, CFA is first, with most members, most cats registered, and most shows. Its membership is spread all over the United States. Challenging CFA in numbers is a relative newcomer, the American Cat Fancier's Association (ACFA), founded in 1955 to give an alternative to the CFA's rigid structure, rules, and format. Its membership is made up of individual fanciers instead of clubs as are ACA and CFA. The Cat Fancier's Federation (CFF), established in 1919, is active largely in the Northeast and Midwest; the International Cat Association (TICA) is the second largest registry in North America. The Traditional Cat Association (TCA) and the American Association of Cat Enthusiasts (AACE) are the new kids on the block, somewhat feisty and very enthusiastic. The Canadian Cat Association is, of course, the Canadian branch of the cat tree.

Some of the above organizations are more receptive to new or experimental breeds than others, setting fewer obstacles in the way of breeders seeking championship status. Several are somewhat regional, as has been mentioned. Some are governed through individual clubs, others by a board of directors, a few by members. Most support, monetarily as well as verbally, medical research, animal shelters, inexpensive neutering clinics, and other animal-centered causes. Some publish a newsletter and/or yearbook with pertinent information records. All train and supply judges for their own shows, which is perhaps second only to the keeping of the pedigree records in importance to the orderly existence of the fancy, since the judge and the breeder together set the visual as well as the verbal standard for the cat.

In order to give an idea of the situation facing a new breed, I have drawn up a chart for a semi-typical fictitious organization.

CATS OF AMERICA INCORPORATED (CAI)

Northeast Regional CAI	SE Regional	NW Regional	SW Regional
Mid-Coast Siamese Breeder Thompson's Valley Cat Club Pine Tree Persian Association Hudson River Feline Fanciers Etc.	Similar	Similar	Similar

Our fictional CAI will be governed by a committe made up of representatives elected or selected by each regional group plus an executive group elected by the entire body. The regional groups will be set up similarly. The small local clubs that make up the regional group may be breeder groups or, as is more usually the case, breeders in one geographic area, each with his or her own breed.

For example, a small local group of Maine Coon breeders in the southeastern section of CAI decide that they would like to show in CAI shows and have more say in decisions regarding CAI's interpretation of the Maine Coon standards. The breeders therefore have a choice—join the local CAI-affiliated club, the Magnolia River Bottom Cat Club, which includes Siamese, Persian, and Abyssinian breeders, or set up a club on their own and then petition to join CAI. They could also perhaps entice the Persian breeders into a Southern Longhairs Associated. Once a member of the large organization, they are then entitled to enter their cats in CAI shows and encouraged to register them in CAI. The inference would be that the Maine Coon breeders would be registering their cats through an association that did not show in their area just so that they would be registered.

To add one more detail to our fictitious central organization, CAI has a registry, of course. When it decides to accept a new breed, it sets certain conditions. The breed is given provisional status. During this time, a required number of cats must be registered with CAI and a breed council set up to cover the breed for the organization. The council is made up of breeders from each regional area plus several members of the governing board. These will agree on the standard that will be used in judging for CAI shows or in those organizations with which CAI has reciprocal agreements. Here endeth the fictional career of CAI.

Because the organizations are so diffuse, diverse, and frequently difficult, and there is no overall governing body, breeders must repeat the recognition process with each organization. It is exhausting to the spirit and often to the purse. Why do it? Because there is no other way to establish a breed in the cat world, and if you want a place in it, you don't try to change it from the outside, hammering at the door.

In addition to the breed councils affiliated with the registry organizations, some breeds have an unaffiliated body that deals nationwide with inquiries and problems, a clearinghouse for matters concerning the breed, an open forum. This is usually made up of breeders who are, at the same time, also members of various breed councils, local clubs, etc. The Maine Coon has one of the best and most dedicated in the Maine Coon Breeders and Fanciers Association (MCBFA), which is large enough to have clout and open-minded enough to publish in its comprehensive and clever *Scratch Sheet* varied and controversial viewpoints, up-to-date medical information from many sources, plus the general in-house information necessary to breeders. There are also state and/or local groups

A basketful of as-yet-unnamed kittens from the Acme Cat Company, showing that. . .
(Photo: Lydia Hynds and Bill Westcott)

the typical Maine Coon kitten, like Angtini's MacGuyver Coon, can be spotted by certain characteristics, one of which being irresistibility . . .
(Photo: Linda Komar)

devoted to the care, breeding, and enjoyment of the cat such as the homegrown Texas Maine Coon-federacy. (Maine Coon people, more than any other group in the fancy, seem to enjoy word games in naming organizations, catteries, and their cats. For further reference, see Chapter 5 and the captions under many of the pictures.)

The diversity between various organizations means that there is no one voice that decides on THE cat. If you would like to read about what sort of trouble having only one registry and overseeing organization can hand breeders and fanciers—and the animals—I recommend you get your hands on the March 1990 issue of *The Atlantic Monthly* and turn to page 49. Mark Derr, in his article "The Politics of Dogs," says it all.

Diversities of philosophy and political structure notwithstanding, the main object of each of these organizations is the keeping of the long genealogical records, the genetic certificate of the purebred. To paraphrase Marshall McLuan, the product is the premise and the product is the pedigreed cat.

and proving once again, as does this bunch of charmers from Texas Belle, that the predominant shade and pattern for Maine Coon kittens is color-me-huggable. (Photo: Phyllis Tobias)

When a potential purchaser sets out to find that dream Maine Coon kitten, he or she has two choices. The first and most obvious is to find a Maine Coon breeder in the area. Breeders of Maine Coons, however, do not regularly advertise in local newspapers, not even one with so large a daily circulation as the New York *Times*. Since they are usually small enterprises with an eye to keeping overhead low, breeders more often advertise in magazines devoted to cats or to pets in general. However, there will be an occasional newspaper ad, usually in conjunction with a show in the area. Shows themselves are great places to meet breeders and talk to them, as well as to see the cats. There are also, of course, breed newsletters, but these are not easily available to the prospective buyer. Maine Coon Breeders and Fanciers has kept up its longstanding tradition of sending to interested parties packets of literature, which frequently include a copy of the newsletter and/or breeder lists. (Further information on this service is included in the Appendix.) Kittens can be shipped all over the country and beyond under a rigid code. Some people make a special trip to the Northeast to pick up their "Maine Coon kitten from the state of Maine," as one breeder puts it.

Why a pedigreed cat? For the breeder, amateur or professional, the advantages are obvious. You know exactly what you have and what you can expect from potential offspring. A kitten from a breeder comes with many extras: a breeder's guarantee of health, a lengthy pedigree from which to deduce the cat's genetic makeup, and a listing of prizes or competitions won by its ancestors. In other words, a pedigree comes as close as you can get to a guarantee that you have a fully representational specimen of the breed in the color and pattern you want. Kittens, like puppies and babies, frequently only give clues, some of them false, to their eventual mature form. With a pedigreed cat, you know what lies ahead. To the average cat owner who does not plan to breed and who may or may not want to show, all these advantages still apply, plus the fact that there is the pedigree to frame.

Pedigreed kittens are generally sold under three categories: household pet, breeder, and show quality. That is not to say that a kitten sold as a household pet might not grow up to be a show-stopper; it is rather to say that the "show quality" kitten is a sure thing. The kitten sold as a household pet is usually sold with the proviso that the owner will have the kitten neutered, after which the breeder will send him the kitten's pedigree. Again, this does not mean that the kitten has any physical defects. It means only that he has traits or potential for traits that would not be considered desirable in the esoteric world of the show ring and that the breeders would not like to see passed on to future generations (e.g., tail a shade too short, small bone structure). To any cat fancier desirous of having the genuine article with papers to prove it and not wishing to incur the potential problems of family planning, this is a number-one bargain, especially since the kitten, when grown, can be shown in the neuter classification maintained by most show organizations. Thus, the owner is not isolated from the social scene of the cat show, which provides a great deal of enjoyment for many owners and some cats. (Actually, the Maine Coon, being rather phlegmatic and enjoying the company of people, is not a bad show cat and can frequently become quite hammy about the whole experience.) A kitten sold as a breeder has excellent potential, a champion or two in its background, and a fine chance of blooming into star quality as an adult. A show kitten is almost guaranteed from the beginning to be a winner.

To the purchaser, it is important to know as much as possible about the breeder. A good one will (1) not overwhelm you with details about show successes and/or prizes; (2) be as careful about getting to know about you as you are about her/him; and (3) often provide you with references. There is sometimes a written promise of registration papers under whatever conditions are laid down by both sides at the time of sale—there should always *be* such an agreement. There are also necessities such as a vet's certificate showing the kitten's health, shots, etc. have been properly attended to, checked, and are up-to-date. All this sounds quite detached and cold-blooded when you are in love, but then so do marriage regulations and certificates. This is, or should be, the basis of a longterm relationship all around, so pay attention.

Prices vary between breeders and in different parts of the country. A few breeders have a one-price structure. More common is a two-price structure that distinguishes between commercial and noncommercial buyers. Others go with the three categories previously mentioned. Prices today have come a long way, all of it up, but then what prices haven't? Any price figures date faster than is believable. It is more sensible to say that you should ask around and try to remain unshockable. Some breeders who are building their stock from foundation may sell second-generation kittens as household pets for much less, with the understanding that they are second generation and the agreement to neuter.

Building from foundation is a concept more central to the Maine Coon's history than that of any other breed. A foundation cat is one that looks like a Maine Coon but has no papers, and its ancestral background is at best speculative. This cat can be registered as a potential foundation cat, usually after having been looked over by several impartial and knowledgeable judges who agree that it fits the standards. The kittens resulting from the mating of a foundation cat with a registered Maine Coon are considered second generation and are carefully watched by the breeder to see that they do not show non-Maine Coon traits. If they do, the foundation papers must be destroyed. If not, the next step is third generation. The degree of registration is rigidly specific. One generation above the lower degree of either parent, thus a foundation cat (first generation), bred to a fully registered Maine Coon could produce only second-generation kittens. These kittens cannot be shown since they may or may not carry recessive characteristics unacceptable in the Maine Coon standard. When this second-generation cat, however, is bred to a registered Maine Coon, the new litter, if the kittens show no off-standard points, is considered to have passed all the filters and to be capable of breeding true. It therefore is a registered Maine Coon.

CFA's Maine Coon Stud Book was closed in the mid-1980s, causing much heated controversy on both sides of the question. Some breeders said quite adamantly that there were too few cats in the gene pool behind the pedigrees and that only by allowing foundation breeding would the Maine Coon keep its characteristics, including the people-y disposition for which it has been noted. On the other side, breeders brought up the fact that breeding from foundation is full of problems, some of them physical, some monetary, some ethical. *Everyone* disagrees on what makes a really good Maine Coon, they say, so how could anyone judge whether or not a foundation cat *was* a Maine Coon or not? If the gene pool is restricted, retorted the other side, we will wind up with the same emphasis on detail that has resulted in problems in the dog world. (They don't mention the Persians who cannot breathe through their pugged noses or anorexic Siamese, but you know that's on their minds.)

The primary edge that the Maine Coon has always had over its brethren in the fancy lies in a combination of foundation registry and the availability of an almost unexploited pool of Maine Coon genetic types in the northeastern states. The practice of building from foundation stock is to this day almost a sure fight-starter in any circle of cat breeders. A great many dedicated breeders, as I have mentioned above, believe that the registered cats are a large enough body to provide healthy bloodlines. They fear, somewhat justifiably, mongrelization of a newly established breed. If foundation registry is honestly abided by, however, there is a constant and monitored influx of new blood, capable of strengthening old traits and breeding out undesirable ones. Foundation cats are usually subjected to much more stringent scrutiny than are cats with known pedigrees, and a combination of dedicated breeders and knowledgeable judges can avoid any relaxing of standards. Judges are more apt to be wary of relaxing standards in the case of a foundation cat than in the case of one whose pedigree reaches back to Willliam the Conqueror of CFA.

After all, as an expert judge once said, "Everybody starts with foundation registry. God doesn't issue pedigrees."

And quite fittingly we now come to the second way to acquire the potential foundation feline, or, in the words of a native Maine neighbor, the "come-by kitten." If you live or vacation in northern New England, this is indeed a possibility. In spring and summer at humane shelters, advertised in the local papers, or announced in hand-lettered signs, many longhaired kittens or "shags" as they are called locally are available for adoption. It is important, however, to know what to look for. In a private home, you can usually see the mother, which will give you a pretty good indication of half of the kitten's genetic inheritance, and occasionally the owner has a pretty good (sometimes profane) idea as to the father. You may also see littermates, which should give you an even better idea, especially if you are familiar with the basics of genetics. This is often not true in shelters, although you may find littermates there. But, if the town is small enough, the person in charge of the shelter sometimes has a good idea of the parentage of the kittens.

Adopting a come-by kitten is not, of course, foolproof. Kittens are not infallible indicators of their adult forms. If you want a sure thing, a breeder is the only way. If you have an adventurous spirit and a low melting point, the come-by kitten will get you every time. Here are a few points to look for.

A Maine Coon kitten at five to six weeks will usually begin to look shaggy as well as fluffy. The tufts in its ears, on top of its ears, and both on and under the paws will be quite apparent, and the thickening neck ruff will begin to appear. The plumy tail will not; it seems to be one of the last characteristics to appear, which it then does overnight in middle kittenhood. The kitten's legs will look sturdy, its paws unusually large, and its ears gigantic. These characteristic exaggerations of the extremities are somewhat less evident in the female, which will be proportionally smaller anyhow, but they will be in evidence. If you are particular about color and patterns, one word of advice. Pale stripes in a kitten often fade out in the adult cat, leaving it a solid color, but if you are that picky about things, a come-by kitten probably isn't for you.

There are several matters that you will probably have to take care of for your come-by kitten that would have been done automatically by a breeder. The kitten will have to be taken to a vet, thoroughly checked to see that it is healthy, and given all necessary shots, including those for feline distemper or panleucopenia. It should also be checked for fleas, earmites, worms or other parasites, and any sign of fungus infection. This visit to the vet is not a luxury; it is a necessity. You will also have to find out on your own what the kitten eats. You may have only a general idea of the kitten's age and can therefore only guess at its stage of development. A good general guide to cat care, and there are many at widely varying prices, is an excellent investment and will give you an idea of what to expect if you have never had a kitten before.

As for the pedantic attitude of people who say, "What in the world kind of cat is that?" this can be simply handled by saying firmly, "He says he's a Maine Coon cat."

Whichever way you get your kitten, the single thing that will affect him most of all is your attitude. Get a kitten because you want one, not because it might be a nice thing to do or because it is decorative or because it might be good for the kids. Taking on a pet is almost as much of a responsibility as taking on a child, and a permanent child at that, although cats often wind up resembling teenagers more than small children. Cats have, unfortunately for themselves, a reputation for being self-sufficient. Perhaps once this was so, but one tearingly sad result in these man-made times is the spectacle of the "temporary" or "vacation" pet, left behind to starve and die without the tools it would have had if it had been wild from birth. Of course, a few survive or find new homes. A great many more don't. When I even think about things like that, I tend to become either tearful or profane or both at once.

"Not needing much care," which, of course, cats don't, has been interpreted as "not needing much attention," which is wrong for most cats and a thorough falsehood for the gregarious and affectionate Maine Coon. Nothing can modify a cat's personality more than neglect. No one would attend to a child's physical needs alone and then expect it to grow to extroverted adulthood. Maine Coons get along well with other household pets as well as people, although they seem to show a decided preference for the company of dogs over that of other cats.

The first Maine Coon I ever saw was sharing the front porch of a small frame house in Round Pond, Maine, with an enormous German Shepherd, side by side. He was gray and white with what I know now to be an incredible ruff, a coat of impressive shagginess, and a tail of impossible proportions. As I went by, he opened his huge golden eyes to give me a lazy once-over and then winked solemnly and snuggled up next to his friend in the sun. I have never seen him since. I don't know if his people know he's a Maine Coon cat or that he would be a surefire winner at the next Portland show or that his ancestors have more stories about them than the five-masted schooners they used to build down this way. But one thing is for sure. He knows who he is.

They all do.

5

Tales
of
the
Cat

Once upon a time, there was a cat . . . .

The Maine Coon character, like that of the
Downeaster, seems a natural spark for all sorts of cat
stories. Just as people from away delight in tales of
the taciturn Mainer and the crafty Vermont native,
so in a group of cat people, you can pick out the
Maine Coon stories by their slightly irreverent, salty
flavor. Some are true folktales in shape and wording,
others are born of ignorance out of misunderstanding,
and still others, usually the more modern, are beautifully anecdotal.

One of the best of these anecdotes is a real Maine
Coon yarn from a breeder whose back-to-basics
daughter spins. The sight of that furry fluff accumu-
lated after the cats' show grooming inspired the
daughter, and she requested that it be saved and sent
to her forthwith. In due time, she presented her parents with possibly the only Maine Coon wool scarf in
existence, in a tasteful Yankee tweed. Use it up, as
the old saying goes; it's good for something.

Two choice portraits from the modern Maine
Coon archives of unusual cats include Socrates
Koppel, a mighty hunter who proudly deposited his
trophies in his owner's piano in a third-floor apartment in Sarasota, Florida, and the Coon kitten from

Zig-Krn's Magnificent Maggie is an example of the Medium-sized Cat in the Large Fur Coat that gives rise to Monster Legends. (Photo: Jim Caparelli)

Poughkeepsie, New York, whose understanding owner's dentist made him a set of braces after an unsuccessful bid for the neighborhood welterweight title.

From San Francisco came the late, lamented, big (but not bad) Leroy Brown, star of stage (King of San Francisco as voted by the public at a big cat show in 1988) and screen (having been driven by limousine—stretch, one imagines—to be featured in *Good Morning, Bay Area*), and winner of enough awards to make him the Mark Spitz of the California cat circuit. His cage was always surrounded by admirers, it is said, and he was irresistible and always mannerly to the ladies, human or feline.

Some Maine Coons have found that, like the milkmaid in the old English ballad, their faces were their fortune. Such was the case of the fluffy kitten that Claire Turlay Newberry obtained through the Central Maine Cat Club and described in her book *Widget*. Many advertisers of cat food and other cat-related products use Maine Coons in their advertising. Examples of this are Monte, a handsome fellow from Florissant, Missouri, whose wicked wink won him a place among the photogenic felines on the *1990 Cat Lover's Calendar*, and Starbuck, a Birmingham, Alabama, resident, whose picture adorns the Gold-Kist Foods' Kitty Kist bags. Gold-Kist's magazine ads seem to feature Maine Coons almost exclusively. After many years of being a mainstay (if you will pardon the pun) of general feline calendars, the Maine Coon now has its very own showcase from LMP of Herndon, Virginia. There is something appealing about the husky, shaggy-coated Maine Coon that finds its target in animal lovers. To quote one letter to MCBFA's *Scratch Sheet* from Ithaca, New York, "The Maine Coon looks like the cat one remembers as a child but never seemed to find again."

Over the past few years in particular, the Maine Coon has gained considerable outside recognition. In April of 1985, the governor of Maine signed a bill (which had been no pussycat to put across his desk) recognizing the Maine Coon cat as the official state feline. It took the overturning of a NO vote from the legislature's State Government Committee (obviously dog-in-the-manger types), and putting up with newspaper headlines like "Coon Cat: The Purr-fect Choice" and "State Committee Tries to Scratch Cat Bill," but the cat won out in the end. HF 199-LC233 made it official and Nonesuch Baxter, a champion Maine Coon and former congressional nominee (with the slogan, "A Maine Coon's Place Is in the House") was there to see it happen, as were many delighted breeders, fanciers, and, of course, suitably gracious cats.

Showcased in 1996 and as much a star as any of those T. S. Elliot-ine CATS was CapeCoon's Boisterous Barron, a headliner in the broadway revival of Irving Berlin's *The Coconuts*. Many fans greeted him at the stage door, his presence was vied for in starred dressing rooms, and he always received an ovation at the end of his performance.

In February of 1988, one of the most charming of the 22-cent commemorative stamps bore the likeness of the Maine Coon as part of a group of eight cats. The stamps sold out, not only in the state of Maine, but there were rumors that dog fanciers were so annoyed that they petitioned their congresspersons, which led to the replacement of the 22-cent stamp by the 25-cent issue.

Then there are tales that illustrate the basic confusions that have surrounded the Maine Coon. In its infancy, MCBFA frequently received letters from sportsmen's magazines and manufacturers of hunting equipment touting devices for, of course, coon hunting. One breeder in Nashville, Tennessee, was contacted by a prospective buyer who wanted to know how Coon cats were as hunters, as he disliked coon hounds. It is not recorded that she made a sale.

The most charming misconception of all, however, is the fable of the "Turquoise" kitten, as it is to this day occasionally advertised. This name has its roots in the era of Captain Clough and the cat from China, Maine, two of the greatest legends in the Coon cat archives, and it rests on the rumor that the cats Captain Clough brought to Maine were Turkish Angoras. Now in French, the word for Turkish is Turquis, and at the time many residents of the extreme northeastern United States spoke French. The theory is that these French-speaking owners of longhaired litters called them Turquis kittens without translating to summer visitors who took them home and called them Turquoise cats, although never a sea-blue kitten resulted. There was a pet shop owner in more modern times who advertised Turquoise kittens for sale. Buyers didn't seem to mind that not one of the kittens was blue-green, that being one of the few colors missing in the Maine Coon spectrum.

Another mythical color, although much less romantic, is the seal-brown or mahogany of the Maine Coons mentioned by early writers such as Frances Simpson in *Cats and All About Them* in 1902. "Among the Maine cats, " she says," are some of a curious seal-brown colour, or a deep mahogany red, with not a vestige or sign of markings." Before this, as noted in Chapter 2, the redoubtable Harrison Weir had passed along similar "information." There is a prosaic and scientific reason for both the appearance and the loss of this color in genetics. In cats, there is a gene called Si, which prevents color from fading or changing due to lengthy exposure to sunlight. Its recessive partner, si, does not prevent this occurrence. Thus, a black Maine Coon, having the recessive form of the gene and being constantly exposed to the sun as all early Maine Coons were since they came and went as they pleased, would turn from its normal black, which is, after all, the darkest of browns, to a seal or mahogany brown. Today's showcats are indoors most of the time, thus diminishing even the chance of a seal-brown Maine Coon.

Equally confusing and even more of a problem to breeders, since the stories crop up occasionally still, are what might be referred to as the physical fallacies. One and all, they have been decisively proven false; yet, like the classic tale of the raccoon/cat cross, they keep surfacing. First is the longstanding myth that Maine Coons are cold-weather Yankees and pine away in warmer areas. This notion persists in the writings of those who should know better, such as Maine adoptee Louise Dickinson Rich. Even the CFA *Yearbook* for 1959 in its section on cats of yesteryear repeats this fallacy, stating that, "the fact that the Maine Cat failed to thrive in warmer climates contributed to its extinction as a breed." Needless to say, this was published prior to the readmittance of the Maine Coon by CFA. Breeders of Maine Coons all over the South and the West can testify to the growing popularity and thriving condition of Coons in their areas.

The early Federal Writer's Project's *Guidebook on Maine* brings up another set of fallacies, referring to Maine Coons as "quite gentle and fragile" in addition to admiring their "long, frosty grey hair" and saying that they are difficult to rear, being particularly susceptible to pneumonia. It is amazing, but authors of cat books today still perpetuate this myth in the face of the sturdy, healthy, colorful Maine Coon. Another equally unfounded assertion comes from an early cat book

The Intrepid Tailspin Tommy and friend. (Courtesy: Vida Grant)

published in Boston, which states that the Maine Coon is "fond of outdoor life and must be allowed to run out-of- doors or it is apt to become so savage and disagreeable that nothing can be done with it."

Of course, legends about the size of the Maine Coon, of concern to many breeders, have been compounded over the years. Truly, the Maine Coon's size, along with its athletic sturdiness, is one of its charms, but reports of this characteristic have undergone the escalation common to all word-of-mouth tales, swelling them into heroic proportions. Most people have no idea what a thirty-pound cat would look like, and the Maine Coon looks bigger than it is anyway with its rectangular conformation and shaggy coat. There do exist Maine Coons of somewhat incredible size to this day, most of them neutered ex-studs. They are, however, few and far between.

But surely the most bizarre physical fallacy story is that the Maine Coon has extra-long hind legs as a result of having two extra vertebrae in its backbone. A veterinarian I know, confronted with this statement, was thrown into spluttering amazement and vehement denial, but the idea was a subject of heated debate between a breeder from New York on the affirmative side, and several Maine natives on the negative in Rockland, Maine's *Courier-Gazette* during December of 1940.

Having brought up the subject of the representation of Maine Coons in newspapers, magazines, and books, mention must be made of the incredibly poor pictures of Maine Coons in magazines of national circulation and reputation until very recently. Even in a magazine like *National Geographic*, the nationally prominent photographer Walter Chandolla came up with pictures of charming felines that showed none of the Maine Coon characteristics. A book by Barbara Michaels, *The Crying Child*, in which Maine Coons play a piquant if minor role, shows a cover cat whose visage is enough to make a Maine Coon breeder consider suing the illustrator.

Some of the stories in the daily papers are worse. The five below get my personal vote for the "Contemporary Award for Seventeenth-Century Journalism."

In September 1973, *Newsday*, a Long Island, New York, daily replied to a question on the Maine Coon with the flat statement, "There isn't any such animal."

In September 1976, in *The Asbury Park Press*, Asbury Park, New Jersey, in a column on pets, Dr. Michael Fox, when asked by a reader as to the family tree of the Maine Coon, didactically stated that the Maine Coon "is merely a large variety of domestic cat that has reverted to the wild."

In July 1977, the *Kennebec Journal* of Augusta, Maine, which for heaven's sake should have known better, in the "Ask Us" column replied to a request for information about white Maine Coon cats with the statement that, "there are no all-white Maine Coons, as their distinctive markings are a dark mask and a ringed tail."

In August 1988, the *Daily Mirror* of London ran a story about "a large domestic breed of cat called the 'Coonmain,'" which was rampaging through the suburb of Edgware.

In April of 1990, the national tabloid *Examiner* ran an article on monster cats, supposedly mutant Maine Coons bred for size and ferocity by unscrupulous breeders, terrorizing lonely farms and towns in New England.

The defense rests.

There is a body of stories, however, that belongs in the true folktale category, modern as well as traditional. Many of these are, of course, from the northeast corner of the United States, since it is here that the breed has been established long enough to evolve the aura necessary to the growth of the folk story. New England also has a love of verbal exchange of stories, a predilection that gives rise to ballads and legends. Those I have collected are given, when possible, exactly as told, most of them anonymously at the request of the tellers.

One of the oldest stories comes from Revolutionary War times, and I have heard it attributed to several places along one or another of Maine's rivers. A family living on Westport Island along the Sheepscot River, one version goes, was close to starvation in the first winter of the war. The father of the household was away fighting, as many Mainers were, and supplies had almost run out. The family was kept alive until spring through the efforts of the household gray shag, which caught and brought home "ice fish" from an open place in the frozen river. These "ice fish" would probably have been smelts, which are caught today by hundreds of Mainers sitting patiently in small, homemade shacks on frozen rivers and lakes, fishing through holes in the ice.

A more modern such fish tale came to me from a lady in Augusta, Maine. "My brother Timothy," she told me, "had a big gray-and-white shag named Commodore Perry who always went fishing with him in the winter. Tim made the Commodore a bed with an old rug on the seat by him and they'd spend days out there fishing. 'Long about the end of the winter one morning, when they'd been fishing awhile, the

Commodore got very funny. He talked and he fussed and he wouldn't let Tim alone. The fish weren't biting too good anyway, so Tim figured he'd take the Commodore home, get himself a hot dinner, and come back in the afternoon. When he did come back, there was a big crack opened up in the river and his shack was gone in it. He always claimed that the Commodore felt that crack starting to work and saved both their lives."

Another elderly lady of my acquaintance remembers Great Eddie, a large Coon cat that "hung out" at the local fish house used for storage and socializing by the lobstermen and fishermen. One summer during a period of storms, so she says, the men were sitting around waiting it out, doing small, necessary gear repairs, swapping stories, and "dampening their throats." They began discussing how much Eddie

Napa Valley Cattery's handsome celebrity the late, great Leroy Brown turns the tables on the paparazzi. (Photo: Patsy Stephens)

weighed, a point on which there were widely varying views since he looked to be such a large percentage of fur. Several wagers were placed on the spot, and Eddie was cajoled into the fish house where they attempted to put him into the scales—a proceeding that did not meet with his approval and was thus rendered impossible. Upon his near escape through an open window, all windows and doors were closed, and the chase was on, made more difficult by the crowded conditions, an uncooperative attitude on the part of several onlookers, and Eddie's athletic ability. By the time he was finally captured and the shed containing several bait barrels had become somewhat stuffy and aromatic, a child was induced to hold up a long-deceased herring so that Eddie would consent to sit quietly and quickly be weighed. My informant was that child, and she remembers that Great Eddie weighed in at forty-two pounds.

Two of the most determined and capable of the Maine Coons or shags, as they are interchangeably called by most older people, are the stars of the classic tale of the cat with the wooden leg and the more modern story of Aunt Sarah's cat. The story of the cat with the wooden leg is typical up-country, and I give it exactly as it was told-for-true to me.

"There was an old fella lived way back and he had him a big old coon cat lived with him for company. It was some fine hunter. The old man didn't have to feed it at all, and mostly it wouldn't even eat what it hadn't caught. So one day the cat caught its foot in a trap, and it turned and it fit so, when the old man finally come upon it, that paw was so chewed and tore about that the old man had to cut off most of the leg. The leg healed up fine but the cat pined away because it didn't like to eat the food it hadn't caught. So the old man whittled out a wooden leg for that cat and a leather harness to hold it on and a leather socket on top so the leg would fit snug and not rub, but fit good. Well, at first that cat amused itself by trying to shake that leg off, but by and by it got accustomed to that leg and could prance around in great fashion. As soon as it got so it could run real fine, it started going into the woods, and the old man saw that the cat was starting to fatten up again. One day he followed upon the cat to see how it managed and he saw that cat creep up on something and grab it with one paw and whack it in the head with that wooden leg. Some old smart, that cat."

70

Aunt Sarah's cat, whose story I heard in a laundromat on a snowy day, was equally determined, if not cast in such a heroic mould. He was, in the words of the gentleman who regaled me with the story but declined to give me his name, "a big, old shag; and he loved Aunt Sarah, followed her around, and made a funny chirpy noise for talking, not a mew like most cats. Aunt Sarah was some demon housekeeper, and she even made that cat wash his feet during mud season before he could come in, or she'd wash 'em for him, and he didn't much care for that so he'd do 'em himself. On occasion, Aunt Sarah would go to see her sister up to Machias and leave Uncle Martin and cat to take care of the house and each other while she was gone. Uncle Martin wasn't much on cleaning, but the day before Aunt Sarah'd come home, he'd set to work and clean up, mostly the kitchen floor, which she was more than particular about. She'd scrub it every other day some seasons. Well, one time Aunt Sarah was gone a week or better, and she came back to find that floor absolutely shiny, it was so clean. Uncle Martin, he claimed that every day or so that cat would tump over something so messy and sticky that he'd have to wash the whole floor fast so the cat couldn't walk in it and track it all over. Claimed he figured Aunt Sarah put the cat up to it. Never was overfond of that cat, Uncle Martin wasn't."

A somewhat more generally acceptable, useful cat belonged to an old lady named Maude Genther. It was a red Coon cat with a white vest and tail tip, and she says he was trained to be a scare cat and keep the crows out of her corn patch. He had a platform in the middle of the corn on which he would sun himself and snooze, occasionally waking up to stretch in a threatening manner. She said she never had any trouble with crows while she had that cat, although there were occasional raids by raccoons. But, she figured the cat and the coons had "an arrangement."

From the early days, Coon cats have been a well-traveled breed. Cats were always welcome on Maine vessels. Coon cats were supposed to be very good at calling up a wind or calming it. They were put on deck under a basket during long calms until "they decided to call the wind back." Mrs. Carroll Grey of Wiscasset, Maine, tells a story about her uncle, Captain Charles Nash of Harrington, Maine, who was in charge of a cargo ship on the West Coast in the 1920's and '30's. Captain Nash had a large, black Maine Coon that was his

Stage star relaxes at Hidden Spa. CapeCoon Baron of Hampton Coon takes his ease after the bright lights of Broadway. (Photo: David Lamberton)

constant companion and cabinmate and an excellent watchcat. The captain swore that, when expanded in anger and vocally threatening, his cat was more frightful than a Doberman. Caesar, another globe-trotting Maine Coon of modern times, visited extensively in the Orient with his army-based people. His views on Siamese were not conducive to amicable foreign relations. The entire cattery of Lt. Col. Connie Condit conducted an instructive blitz of German cat shows during her tour of duty in Europe.

Perhaps the most exotic traveler of all these peripatetic felines, however, was Yankee Clipper, the cat who penetrated the Iron Curtain. On April 12, 1972, in a sturdy, wooden crate, this intrepid black-and-white Maine Coon kitten started on a 6,000-mile journey from New York to Bucharest, Romania. The crate was literally covered with signs and pictures—cats, an American flag, MCBFA and other cat-organization emblems, to say nothing of labels in all potentially useful languages telling officials that this was live baggage. He was outweighed by the pile of forms including health certificates, pedigrees, and other documentation, and he was visaed, vouchered, and notarized in several languages. This was a through flight, so he would not have to change planes. Amazingly enough, all went well, and his new family picked him up at the Bucharest airport at 5:30 the next afternoon.

Tailspin Tommy, another inveterate traveler, went everywhere with his owner, Vida Grant, one of the first licensed women pilots in the state of Maine. An article about his cross-country trips appeared in the November 1946 issue of the magazine *Yankee Pilot* and included a picture of Tommy at his handsome best. Regrettably, Tommy was not shown wearing his regulation helmet in the plane, which he flew with some assistance.

His story, however, does not stop there and leads into a field with which cats have been associated since time immemorial, the supernatural. Tailspin died, a victim of DDT poisoning, and was buried in a corner of the family plot, so the story goes, with a small, unmarked stone of his own. A year or so later, there began to appear on that stone the outline of a cat regally seated with a large, fluffy tail curled neatly about his paws, a posture often adopted by Tailspin, who had a tail to make a Persian green with envy.

An even stranger story comes from a lady in Skowhegan, Maine, whose twenty-year-old Maine Coon had always hated the sound of her grandfather clock. Frequently, she said, he contrived to get at the chains and weights and stop it, and he never stopped glaring at it when it chimed the hour. The night he died, she told me, she dreamed that he came back, floated in the air up to the face of the clock, and stopped the hands at seven. The next morning when she awoke, sure enough, the clock had stopped at seven, and she was never able to get it to run again.

The story of Miss Lucinda Ware's cat, told me by a charming elderly lady in a nursing home, is another return story with a happy ending. "Miss Lucinda's cat was a big, gold-colored shag named Buddy of whom she was very fond and who followed her everywhere, even in the garden. When he died at the age of eighteen, she was most inconsolable and cried and carried on and mourned like one of her family had passed over. She swore she would never have her another cat, and she didn't for a long time. Then one day during a rainstorm, there come up on her porch a half-grown kitten, gold with dark orange stripes, and meowed to be let in. He was all scraggly and scruffy and thin as a pencil and she couldn't resist him, so she let him in— only for a while, she said, until she could find out who he belonged to. Of course, he took up his residence, and when he grew big, his tail fluffed out and his coat got all long and shaggy. But the strangest thing of all was that his stripes all went away as he grew up, until when he was grown, he was all golden and looked the image of Buddy. So she called him Buddy-boy and he lived to be twenty-three years old, which is some age even for a shag."

Maine Coons seem to specialize in the inexplicable. Everyone knows, for example, that calico males, short- or long-haired, are few and far between, and those few are sterile. A retired railroad engineer once had such a Maine Coon, a striking calico male he called John D. Rockefeller, since calico cats are also known as "lucky money cats" or just "money cats" in many parts of New England. Being a widower, he used to soliloquize to John D. on the unfairness of their being excluded from the increase of their breeds, he because of his age and John D. because of his sterility. It must, he figured, have really riled John D. because one day he disappeared and was gone for several weeks, returning with a charming and obviously quite pregnant small gray female of indeterminate ancestry. The engineer, who was living with his married daughter at the time, was amused by what he considered a transparent ruse and talked his daughter into sheltering the mother cat and trying to find homes for her and the prospective kittens. When the kittens finally arrived, everyone was amazed and incredulous; there were two long-haired calicos in the bunch. A vet they consulted said it was impossible and a mere coincidence. John D., however, just sat there looking smug and washing the kittens.

But the most widely known and the most variedly told of all cat tales in the state of Maine is the story of the cats of Haskell's Island, and it is a most fitting and proper end to this study of the Maine Coon in fact and fiction. Haskell's Island had at one time, to give the legend its traditional beginning, belonged to an old fisherman named Haskell, whose demise had been due to the huge and fearless rats that inhabited the island. After his death, cats were brought in by two young fishermen from North Harpswell, Wallace and Bruce Mills. They began living on the rat-infested island against the advice of their peers, using it as a base for lobstering. The cats they brought over were described as "big, strong, old shag cats" and, like Dick Whittington's cat of another era, they declared war on the rodent population and won. The cats thereupon became quite prolific and extremely protective of their turf. The only people they would allow on the island were the Mills boys, but that was quite all right with Wallace and Bruce because they didn't much care for people messing about near their camp in their absence anyhow. One day a summer visitor who intended to buy the island came out; finding the Mills boys at home, he informed them that they were squatting on land he planned to own and ordered them off. After enlightening them as to their lack of rights, he proceeded to attempt to explore the island. The cats chased him off—cheered on one imagines, by the brothers. The man came back the next time the brothers went out to haul their traps, set out poison for the cats, and killed every one. The brothers buried their cats and left the island, brokenhearted.

Most versions simply stop there. Others say that for some reason the man never bought the island and that no one has seen a cat or a rat on it from that day to this. But by pure luck, I stumbled on a more complete ending, which, true or not, rounds the legend off in a much more fitting fashion.

The same gentleman who told me the story of the cat with the

75

wooden leg and several others, and whom I consider a lineal if not genealogical descendant of the "local source" of the tale of the cat from China, Maine, filled me in on this one after I had regaled him with the stories I had collected in my research. When I recounted the above version of the cats of Haskell's Island, he chuckled. "That story's got more versions than they've got black flies up-country," he said. "Some of 'em, the boys are named Haskell and some of 'em, the cats ate old man Haskell, and once I even heard that's where shags started, because a bunch of wild cats was shipwrecked on that island by a crazy man named Haskell who was trying to ship them to some zoo. But the one you've got is pretty much the one I've heard the most, so it's either the neatest or the truest." He filled his pipe and regarded me over the flame as he lit it. "You know, Sis," he said finally, and his voice had that slow, musical cadence that comes to all born storytellers when they have just found a fresh and receptive ear for an old favorite, "you don't have the whole end of it . . . ."

"It seems that the summer fella and a group of his friends came out to the island early that next fall to fish and stay a night or two. He hadn't bought it yet, just optioned it, but he treated it like he owned it and marched around showing it off and burned down the old shack the Mills boys had lived in. He and his friends, they set up some tents, and they planned out where his house ought to go and all the parties they would throw, and by and by the sun started going down. They made up a fire out of drift wood and sat around it, but the fire made the darkness around even darker, and they started hearing funny noises and rustlings back in the dark and the bushes. When they went into their tents, they couldn't sleep for the sounds, and anytime they went out, there were shining eyes watching them from the dark and things moving out there that were gone if you shone a light and things pushing at the tent that were gone when you got outside. The summer fella went out and he sat by the fire with his shotgun, but there was nothing to shoot at, just the feeling of something watching you and seeing something moving out of the corner of your eye and nothing there when you looked at it straight. So they didn't stay to fish but went away early the next morning, and he never bought the island, and there are fishermen and lobstermen to this day that'll stay there and others that won't."

And the cat wins again.

6

On
Peaceful
Coexistence

Maine Coon cats are among the most companionable of felines. The following chapters, while containing a few specifics, will give you an idea of what is necessary from you in regard to life's basics: food, shelter, grooming, education (mainly yours), and health care, not only for your Maine Coon but for any cat who shares your life. Some items are negotiable; some aren't. In matters of individual taste, you can hash it out together. The important thing is to get these basics straight in your mind right away so that the cat cannot bluff you into thinking it knows best. And the first order of things, possibly the most important to the owner, is nutrition.

Cats have a largely unjustified reputation for being finicky eaters. Frequently, this may be due less to the taste of the food than its temperature, since most cats dislike eating their food direct from the refrigerator. Cats are, however, unusual in their nutritional requirements, needing and being capable of assimilating more protein per pound than other animals and having less tolerance for carbohydrates.

"From a metabolic point of view," to quote Dr. Sandford Miller, professor in the Department of Nutrition and Food Science at Massachusetts Institute of Technology, "the cat is truly unique." For the cat, this fact has led to problems. Little study was done in the field of feline nutrition simply because it had little or no correlation to human nutrition or even to that of other animals, connections that might have opened the way to federal or private grant funding. Pet food companies, to be sure, have done research for many years, but often from a commercial point of view and with an eye to increasing the palatability of the food rather than from a nutritive viewpoint. The result was what is still referred to in some circles as "the great red tuna scandal" of about twenty years ago, when many cats were fed wholly or chiefly on canned food made from this high-fat fish, the chocolate of the cat world. A diet of this kind resulted in steatitis or yellow fat disease, a painful inflammation of the cat's body fat due to vitamin E deficiency. The cat's stores of vitamin E are depleted in digesting unsaturated fat, which red tuna contains in great quantity. Once this situation was diagnosed, pet food manufacturers began adding supplemental vitamin E to the product, but the whole episode served as the introduction to a new era in pet food supervision.

Until the 1960's, there was no regulation of pet food manufacturers' labeling or advertising claims. In 1962, the National Academy of Sciences' National Research Council established guidelines for the nutritional care of laboratory animals, and work began toward proper labeling and regulation of advertising. In 1969, a Federal Trade Commission guide was established, requiring rigid standards for pet foods labeled "complete," "scientific," or "balanced" and more complete nutritional information on labels, thus relieving the purchaser of the absolute necessity of spending hours with the fine print on the side of box, bag, or can.

Commercial cat foods, like all Gaul, are easily divided into three parts: dry, moist, and canned. With a little knowledge of their good and bad points, the owner can easily and satisfactorily rely on nothing more if desired.

DRY. The adult cat needs a minimum of twenty-one percent protein and seven to eight percent fat in the ration if fed nothing but dry cat food. Fat may be added quite easily, if the ration is otherwise well balanced and the cat likes it, by adding one tablespoon of cooking oil or bacon fat. Meals can also be moistened with milk or broth. Kittens need the same amount of fat, but their protein level must be thirty-three percent.

The advantages of dry food are: 1) it is cheaper, 2) self-feeding is possible, 3) dry food provides good exercise and abrasion for cleaning teeth and gums, an element cats lack otherwise since they are not, in civilization at least, bone chewers. The chief problem seems to be a higher incidence of urolithiasis (kidney stones) or cystitis (bladder inflammation and/or infection) in cats fed solely on dry food. This, however, is a matter of debate and conjecture, so there are adamant believers on both sides of the question among owners and veterinarians.

Moist. Often more palatable to cats than dry food, this extensively advertised relative newcomer to the cat-food market is more expensive than the dry chows but less expensive and much neater than canned. I personally consider it a product on a par with the disposable diaper. This type of food often has a high phosphorus content, which disposes toward urolithiasis, plus artificial moisture retainers, plus sugar. I think it is aimed at owners who feel guilty about feeding a pet dry food but still want to be economical.

Canned. Canned foods are more expensive, loudly preferred by cats in general, and the oldest type of commercial cat food. "Complete" foods are, of course, excellent diets for cats. Be sure you read the labels, though, for "complete" and "balanced" are two different things. However, if the only imbalance is fat, less than 5 percent, that can be added as with the dry.

There are two rather importanat DON'Ts here. DON'T always feed the same brand, the same flavor. Cats are inclined to develop narrow food preferences easily, a fact that led directly to the legendary finicky cat. If brought up from kittenhood onward to enjoy a variety of tastes and textures, the cat is much better off. DON'T leave canned cat food out long after mealtime. Mythology to the contrary, cats are not natural nibblers. Like their cousin, the lion, cats prefer to eat one large meal at a time.

There are also prescription diets in many varieties to be specified by your veterinarian in case of illness or physical deficiency.

There are many feline physical ailments that are now considered caused by diet, and these can often be alleviated or sometimes cured by a change in what your pet eats. Your vet will be up on the latest, so ask him or her. There are also truly informative and up-to-date newsletters to which you can subscribe (or talk your local library into doing so). These cover topics of both daily life and medical importance to vets, owners/breeders, and—of course—cats. In addition, they are often very interesting reading all around. There are several examples given in the Appendix, which come with recommendations from breeders and owners.

To summarize, dividing your cat's ration into some dry and some canned food is sensible as a general rule. When feeding dry cat food as a major portion of the diet, be sure to make water available at all times. Cats exclusively fed on canned food get 75 percent of their moisture from their food. Read the label if this figure sounds high.

Many people feed their cats a large percentage of regular "people" food, however, and some totally dispense with the commercial pet products. Should you fall into this category, here are a few less-well-known facts and pointers.

MILK is not well tolerated by all adult cats nor even by a few kittens. Often a cat that cannot digest milk can and will eat yogurt, particularly if the cat is ill and cannot handle solid foods. Cottage cheese is also an excellent sourse of digestible protein. Cheese, although many cats adore it, tends to be binding if fed in quantity. I have never met a cat who didn't like ice cream, usually vanilla.

EGGS, regardless of your grandmother's advice, are not good for cats or dogs raw; at least the white is not. Cooked, the whole is digestible and another good source of protein.

FISH, against all you've ever heard, should be cooked, just to be on the safe side, since some raw fish contains an enzyme that destroys thiamine.

MEAT, whether better raw or cooked, has always been a matter of controversy, basically depending on the age and kind of meat. With meat prices these days, however, the only meat your cat is likely to get is leftovers from dinner, which rather does away with the debate. Liver can be fed to cats at the rate of about one ounce twice a week. Too much liver can produce excessive vitamin A, which can cause diarrhea. Bones are not a good idea for cats, another myth being that cats can somehow magically digest small, sharp, splintery bones. Most cats are thoroughly bored by the kind of bones that are permissible, such as beef or leg of lamb; they adore the ones that are dangerous, like chicken, chop, or rib, and will even raid garbage cans for them. Frequently, nothing is upset except the neighborhood order, but it can be pretty unpleasant and sometimes fatal for the cat when bones lodge in the small intestine.

GREENS are another debatable point. Some cats seem to crave them, others regard them as a small boy does spinach. There are, I am told, cats who live long, healthy lives on vegetarian diets, although I am sure they are cases of accommodating cats and determined owners. On this score, I am inclined to go with the cat's personal preference—I once had a cat who was mad about broccoli. Indoor plants are another story, which will be taken up in more detail later. Many apartment dwellers grow a small pot of wheat or oats for their indoor cats to keep them out of the other plants and vice versa. Sometimes it works and sometimes it doesn't.

VITAMINS AND MINERALS are necessary for the cat as they are for people, but felines have special needs. Cats, for example, need vitamin A because they, unlike most animals, cannot manufacture vitamin A from green vegetation. If there is an oversupply of vitamin A, however, they are unable to store it. Calcium and phosphorus should be present in the diet of cats in the ratio of one to one. This balance, if upset, results in demineralization of bone. In addition, vitamin D must be present in sufficient quantity to make the whole alchemy work. (For those interested in looking further into these and other nutritional matters, I have included in the Appendix reference sources that go into further detail, including charts and tables.)

As to those important concerns about when and how much to feed, individual cats differ, not only due to their environment and amount of exercise, but to their metabolism. Be guided on the amount by the suggestions on the container and keep an eye on your cat's shape. On the following page is a simple and handy table with which to begin if you get eyestrain from supermarket label reading.

TABLE FOR FEEDING AND CARE OF THE CAT

Courtesy: Lon D. Lewis, D.V.M, Ph.D., Associate Professor
Mark L. Morris Chair in Clinical Nutrition
Colorado State University

Characteristics of Forms of Commercial Cat Foods

Form	Sold in	Energy content	Needed daily for maintenance*	Percent water	Percent protein	Percent fat
					in the dry matter	
Dry	Sacks	200-300 kcal/cup	1 cup	10	33	8-10
Soft-moist	1-1/2 oz. pkg.	125 kcal/pkg.	2 pkgs.	30	41	11-13
Canned	12-15 oz. can	250-300 kcal/can	1 can	75	40-95	8-24
	6 oz. can	165-225 kcal/can	2 cans	75	40	8-10

*Average amount needed daily for the eight-pound housecat. Increased amounts are needed during pregnancy, lactation, and growth.

Normally, cats prefer to eat once a day, but they can easily get into the habit of eating when you do. If that happens with your approval, portion the rations accordingly. A fat cat is neither happy nor healthy, and while obesity is not a general problem with cats, it is certainly possible. About that old controversy, whether neutering does or does not cause animals to get fat, I reserve judgment. But neutering does seem to set off some chain reaction by which the animal becomes much hungrier, and if this is indulged and exercise not increased, we all know what that leads to—canine, feline, or human.

One more thing. Do not feed your cat dog food. A cat is a cat is a cat.

Grooming is largely done by the cat. Of all the long-haired breeds, the Maine Coon is the most nearly self-grooming, but not to the extent many people think. Normal shedding occurs in spring and fall, but many cats seem to shed perpetually, particularly indoor cats and longhairs. In addition, there are potential tangles. A comb in time often saves cutting out a truly Gordian knot. Here, reprinted with permission from MCBFA's *Scratch Sheet* of Spring 1978, is Connie Condit, longtime breeder and columnist-in-residence, on the subject of grooming. It contains in succinct and amusing fashion everything you always wanted to know on the subject and felt silly about asking.

POT PURRY

I've had a number of requests for advice on grooming Maine Coon Cats. With the "Spring Shed" just a few weeks away, this is a good time to review the procedure, or at least the one I use.

Let's first establish a few facts. The Maine Coon is not a Persian. He has a coat that is more or less self-grooming. He does shed and during periods of heavy shedding, he may matt. However, on most Maine Coons the matts are small, comparatively loose, and will tend to work themselves out away from the skin and eventually drop off—on the furniture, in the soup, etc. This being the case, why bother to groom at all?

Well, if you don't, you will have fur not only in your soup but all over everything. Furthermore, puss will look like a moth-eaten muff and will decorate your happy home with burped hair balls as well as hair. Second fact: the finished product should be a cat with an essentially clean cut top line flowing down into "fringed" underpants. He should not look fluffy! Even his bib appears "tailored" when compared to a Persian.

To achieve this, you need just two combs—no "hair tonic," no powder, no brush. A brush is really rather useless; it just skims the surface and fools you into thinking your cat is well groomed, while underneath is a mass of dead hair. One comb should be a "flea comb" with 21 teeth per inch. This is for the short fur on head, shoulders, and legs. The other should be a standard wire comb with 12 teeth per inch. I like the type with a wooden handle best. If your cat has a very heavy coat you might want to add a second one of these with 9 teeth per inch.

Some cats like grooming; some like it until you reach the britches; and some raise Holy Ned if you even reach for a comb. Since I have some of each, I give myself an edge on the protesters by using a formica top grooming table—no traction for fast take-offs. It is also a comfortable height and by having a specific place for grooming, it conditions puss (for better or worse) to know what to expect when he is put there.

Begin combing at the head with the flea comb. This feels good (even to the rebels) and puts puss in a good mood for the rest. If there is a lot of pull with this comb, switch to your 12 tooth comb for the first combing and then back to the flea comb. Whenever one comb seems to be pulling excessively, switch to a comb with fewer teeth.

Work from front to back and from top to bottom. If an area has a matt, work from the outside into the skin in short strokes, catching just a bit more of the matt each time. Almost any matt can be worked out this way without causing puss too much discomfort. If there are no matts, comb out from the skin. Pay particular attention to the "arm-pits" and flanks. My kids have learned to allow me to stretch their "arms" up so I can comb from under the arm down the side to the flank. Underparts can be combed with the cat standing or held in a sitting position with his back braced against you.

To comb the britches, I tuck puss under my left arm, Mammy Yokum style, and hold him firmly against me with my upper arm. This leaves my left hand free to stretch and hold the back legs. Matts often form just above the hock and if puss flexes his legs, you can't reach them. This is also a good time to do the tail, working from base to tip. Be particularly thorough under the base of the tail.

With just a minimum of once a week grooming, your Maine Coon will be in show condition all the time and you can eat your soup with-out saying "Ptoooey"!

As far as bathing goes, there are experts who say never and others who say it's perfectly all right as often as you and the cat feel like it. It is generally agreed, however, that, if a bath is necessary due to the cat's illness or its falling into something awful and smelly, certain pro-cedures are necessary to make the experience tolerable and safe for both participants. Bathing does not cause illness; becoming chilled is the danger. Long-haired cats should be combed out before bathing to avoid worse tangles later. If you don't want to buy a special cat sham-poo, and if your cat has no specific skin problem that requires a medi-cated shampoo (in which instance, you would, of course, consult your vet), baby shampoo is the thing to use, and for long-haired cats a little creme rinse afterward, thoroughly rinsed out. This tip makes the later-day tangle simpler to remove. A rather clever idea is to put a small window screen or a rubber tubmat such as those used for babies in the bottom of the tub for the cat to cling to. Most important: have the room warm, dry the cat completely afterward, keep it out of drafts, and don't let it go outside for several hours.

Tar, paint, and heavy oil are real problems. Don't use gasoline, tur-pentine, paint remover, nail polish remover, or anything with acetone. Soaking the fur with vegetable oil or mineral oil aids in removal; fol-low up by washing with soap and water, then snipping out any stub-born clumps. Lighter oil is more easily removed by sprinkling with cornstarch or fine cornmeal, which is then combed out of the fur.

If the cause of the problem was a skunk, a tomato-juice rub followed ten minutes later by a water rinse will help. Nothing solves the problem completely except abstaining from the company of skunks.

Do not put perfume on cats. They don't like it on themselves, although they may enjoy sniffing it on you.

Use mineral oil or unscented baby oil on a piece of cotton for cleaning the inner corners of the eye and the ear interstices if necessary. Check, don't just mess about. Most cats keep their ears clean with no help at all and need just a touch in the corner of the eye on occasion.

Those sharp things, claws and teeth, need a bit of outside help. Some cats bite their nails; others use trees, scratching posts, or your favorite petit-point footstool. A great help toward avoiding this dilemma and actually helping your cat, which does not enjoy going around like the neighborhood Chinese mandarin, is a nail clipper for pets, available at your local pet store. Be sure it is sharp.

With many cats, a clipping of the claws is better attempted as a two-person job. It can also be accomplished with a recalcitrant client by using a large, well-tucked-in towel as a temporary strait jacket. As to the actual act of clipping, extend the claw by placing your index finger on the pad of the toe in question and your thumb over the top of that toe and then squeeze your fingers gently together. Look at the claw carefully and you will see that most of it is translucent, and through it you can see an enclosed pink center. The claw itself will hook, rather like a crescent, and you simply cut off the hooked part where it turns, staying away from the pink. If you do accidentally hit the pink part, it will bleed, you will feel awful, and the cat will swear loudly. If this happens, apply a styptic pencil and don't let the cat outside until the claw heals. The cat, after this, will be exceedingly reluctant to have a manicure, and you will be much more careful where you cut.

I shall not even discuss declawing. I consider it an unnecessary act that creates major problems for the cat while eliminating only minor inconveniences for the owner.

Teeth are not usually a problem, particularly if part of the cat's diet is made up of dry cat food, which retards formation of plaque and tartar. That's right, just like people. If you are really upset by the looks of your cat's teeth, and/or the cat has bad breath, you can clean the outer surfaces yourself with a gauze pad moistened with water. Goodness only knows how your cat will react.

Kittens replace their baby teeth between three and five months. I have to take this on faith because I have never observed it, the phenomenon being less obvious in kittens than in children.

Now that the cat is neat and well fed, we turn to something I will call, for want of a better word, lifestyle, the everyday bits and pieces of living.

With cats, as with everything else that lives with you, the trick is to begin as you mean to go on. "Just this once" doesn't count, and "no" must always mean "no." A firm "no" when the cat is caught in the act and immediate removal from the scene works with many cats. A jet of water from a water pistol is frequently even more effective as a surprise deterrent. The key to success is to decide on as few out-of-bounds acts as possible and stick to them. Expecting a cat to live in a Victorian parlor surrounded by "knockoverables" is somewhat naive, although I have known cats who pulled it off as if they were the queen herself.

Housebreaking is the least of problems with cats. The litter box should be an easy-to-clean plastic or baked enamel pan filled two inches deep with any commercial cat litter. It should be kept clean, needless to say; solid matter should be removed daily, and the litter changed as needed. The box should always be in the same place.

Kittens almost come housebroken if the mother is. A new kitten must be shown the litter box, placed in it, and then allowed to climb out to go exploring. Nine times out of ten, that is the end of that. The tenth time, the kitten must just be placed in the box after each meal until the idea is natural. If the kitten is to go outdoors as well, it will catch on to that itself and thus become ambidextrous as it were, although I had a Siamese that for years would dig happily in the garden but come indoors to use her litter box.

If your cat makes a mistake, don't rub the cat's nose in it. This just doesn't work with cats. Say "no" loudly and place the cat in the litter box.

A mistake made by a grown, housebroken cat is either a sign of illness or a strong statement that there is a problem to which the cat wishes to call your attention. The problem may be: "my litter box is not clean," "nobody is paying any attention to me," or "someone else is using my litter box." (Some will accept this latter, some won't.) Whatever it is, look for the illness or the problem for a long time before you decide the cat is incorrigible. If the cat makes a mistake on something nondisposable, try one of the commercial stay-away sprays if you can stand it.

Maine Coon kittens, when they are brought to their new home, should be at least six to eight weeks old and weaned. The kitten whose mother has died or has abandoned it, the former being the more general case, can be raised by hand, but it takes an incredible amount of time and effort and holds several pitfalls for the human surrogate. Feeding is not really one; everyone knows the doll's bottle or eyedropper feeding method. But the surrogate parent must also teach the kittens to use the litterbox, to eat from a dish, and to wash themselves, all of which take time and patience. For formulas and further details, I recommend books with some explicit detail, such as those mentioned in the Appendix.

Many times, people will take two kittens to keep each other company. This is a great deal of fun, both for the kittens and the owner. I myself prefer one at a time, because the kitten seems to grow up to be more people-oriented, but that is a personal choice. Other pets are more tolerant of a newcomer that enters as an infant, although it may take quite a while to establish the pecking order to everyone's agreement if not satisfaction. As a precaution, all claws should be clipped prior to introductions. I have known the establishment of cordial relations to take six months, so don't be discouraged if it isn't love and kisses after a few weeks.

Children and pets are another combination presenting great potential for charm and equally great potential for unpleasantness. Since it is easier to explain things to kids than to kittens, the rules should be laid down in that order. Children should be taught how to play with the kitten (gently), when to leave the kitten alone (often), and how to pick the kitten up, which is not a bad thing to teach adults, too. Don't pick up a kitten by the scruff of its neck or let it dangle or hold it around its tummy. The correct procedure supports the entire body, usually bringing it in to your body for warmth, and the grip is firm but not tight. Problems that seem to require personal intervention on your part should, for the most part, be avoided. For example, how do you get a cat out of a tree? Don't, unless it is a tiny kitten, and even then give it a chance to come down on its own. How do you stop a cat fight? Pour cold water over all participants.

It is also a good idea to teach the cat early in your relationship either its name or a special call-noise to which you want it to respond by coming. Bear in mind that this will not be as reliable a procedure as it is with dogs, but cats will and do come to some sort of call. If coming is rewarded and reinforced in kittenhood, cats will respond, and the whole thing will be very handy in emergency situations. Make it a game with a kitten; don't wear it out, and it will serve you both well.

Cats and plants, as mentioned earlier, pose problems, not only to the plants and their containers, but often to the cat as well. The plant-eating cat is usually a bored indoor cat. The general hypothesis about why cats eat grass is to clean out their stomachs or to aid in getting rid of hairballs. This has never been proven. Some cats, however, just seem to be fond of salad. I have mentioned growing them some, and I have heard of discouraging extracurricular munching by putting a little cayenne pepper on off-limits plants. The eating of some houseplants may be annoying to the owner; the eating of others may be dangerous, if not fatal, to the cat. Here are a few potential botanical Borgias: philodendron, English ivy, dieffenbachia (dumb cane), and just about anything in the flowering-bulb line. (Cat-care books listed in the Appendix have fuller lists.)

The cat's idea of what constitutes a toy, like the preference of a small child, is rarely what you expect it to be. Just as the child would sometimes rather play with a lid and a spoon than a gorgeous educational toy, a cat will often ignore a "cat toy." My cats' preferences in the toy line have been pipe cleaners twisted into spirals, rings from milk-container tops, and ping-pong balls.

As far as hunting goes, cats seem to catch mice without being taught. They also, unfortunately, catch birds, squirrels, and your pet fish if not discouraged. I have read that cats can be taught not to catch birds, but I have never come upon any description of how this might be done. The bell on the collar has always seemed a dubious ploy for me, for it has never been proven that the bell is a warning to birds. Most cats on the prowl move so smoothly that the bell does not ring, and it might on occasion call the cat's presence to the attention of some larger animal hunting the cat.

Cats are eclectic about where they sleep except for one thing; they want to choose it. If you emphatically do not want your cat to sleep with you, make that clear from the beginning. Provide a bed. It can be as elaborate as one of those Marie Antoinette or Scarlett O'Hara types the fancy pet stores sell or as simple as a cardboard box lined with something soft and malleable. Perhaps three out of five cats will accept this; the rest will find their own resting place. However, be warned that it will probably be the back of your knee after you have gone to sleep and are incapable of ejecting the cat. In such a position, an eight-pound cat can turn itself into an anchor and pin down the covers. I have even heard of cats who used their cat carriers as beds—a real boon to their owners since the animals are thus accustomed to a necessity. And that brings up the next topic, travel.

The cat carrier may look like a small suitcase (excellent for smuggling in a quiet cat), a miniature peaked-roofed barn, or a giant, old-fashioned lunch box with a clear plastic top. It is, sensibly enough, a device for transporting a cat from place to place with a chance at maximum mutual tranquility, and for many cats it is the only way they are transportable. Cats in general do not enjoy traveling and would much rather stay home with a house-and-cat-sitter if you are going on a long trip. On the other hand, they usually dislike boarding out, being creatures of habit and fond of their own hearthside.

If you are taking your cat with you in the car and if the cat is permitted to roam about, someone had better have a restraint close at hand (a leash to clip to collar or harness, for example) and an extra hand or two to extract the cat from the least accessible place in the car, which is usually where the cat will go. Taking an unrestrained and uncontained cat anywhere in a car alone is next to impossible and risky even with the most well-behaved cat. Also, never take an inexperienced traveler even around the block without some kind of litter-box provision. The inconvenience is miniscule compared to the unpleasantness that can occur and, by Murphy's Law, does if you are not prepared.

Another necessity is a collar or harness with an easily and quickly attachable leash and some form of identification tag with your name (not the cat's) and address on it. I have seen cats walking regally and impressively on a leash, but there was always the feeling that it was, on the cat's part, a pure indulgence accorded a much-loved owner. Leash training is a good idea to try, however. Some cats will be trained, and some won't. For traveling, the restraint is a necessity, since a frightened cat loose in unfamiliar territory is almost impossible to corral and not much easier to hold.

A traveling cat is usually a frightened cat, and it frequently refuses to eat. Water is a necessity and should be offered at every opportunity.

If the cat is traveling alone by train or plane, it is up to the owner to check and double-check the route and all arrangements. Cats can and do make trips like this safely and neatly, but it is never easy for anyone. If there are too many changes, the chances of a cat's being left somewhere mount, the thought of which is enough to traumatize an owner, let alone a cat. When possible, avoid such trips.

The upshot of this whole discussion is, I suppose, as follows: There are cats who enjoy traveling, and there are cats who loathe it. Find out which you have and act accordingly.

And then there are cat shows. Having discussed briefly in Chapter 4 the organizations of the cat-show world, I shall try to look at the whole procedure for a minute from the owner's point of view, if not the cat's.

Perhaps of all the breeds, Maine Coons seem to enjoy or at least tolerate the show fuss best. I hasten to add that this is not true across the board, but generally. Coon cats seem more at ease and frequently inclined toward hamming it up. Many of the judges to whom I have talked consider them a pleasure to handle, once they stop being intimidated by the sheer amount of cat. One judge even calls them "the gentle giants of the cat world." I can only surmise that Maine Coon owners and breeders tend to play with, talk to, and handle their cats a great deal, considering them as personalities rather than types, and that the cats are therefore amenable to being handled because they are used to it. This quirk is also sincerely appreciated by your local vet.

For the owner who wants to show, here are a few tips to make everybody's life easier. If you plan to show your Maine Coon, get the cat used to 1) being groomed, 2) traveling, and 3) being handled by strangers. Cats who bite judges do not get good marks for strong teeth. *Cat Fancy*, a monthly magazine, regularly lists cat shows all over the U.S. in chronological order for that month and about four ahead, giving information on types of cats to be shown and sponsoring organizations, complete with when and where and whom to contact. The owner then writes to the given name to ask for an entry blank and show flyer. It is also a good idea to ask for a copy of the show rules of the sponsoring organization, because it is up to the individual entering to know and abide by them, and they differ from one organization to the next. There are also web sites providing this information for the computer literate. Several of these will be listed in the Appendix and will probably lead you to others.

The first time you add a cat to your household, there are many things you don't know and the cat can't tell you. This chapter is intended to give you a running start in everyday matters. After a while, you will begin to learn the cat's "language," and it will learn yours, although there will be times of feigned ignorance. The only hurdle left will be medical problems, covered in the next chapter.

7

The
Home
Paramedic
and the
Impatient
Patient

If you're lucky, you may rarely need to use this
chapter, but read it anyway—if ever you do need it,
you had better be able to find what you want fast.
Just as every home should have a well-thumbed first
aid book, so every pet owner should have the animal
equivalent right alongside it. With this chapter, the
attempt will be to provide an overall view of possible
problems and solutions. It is strongly recommended,
however, that you also own a copy of one of the more
complete guides on the subject. These books do not
attempt to substitute for your local veterinarian, but
they can tell you what to do until you get there and/
or some of the things you can handle yourself.
Murphy's Law, the one that says that bread always
falls butter-side down, has a corollary: if you are prepared for it, it doesn't happen. This is known in some
circles as the Murphy's Umbrella Corollary.

The most important considerations in health care,
human or animal, are home safety and preventative
medicine. Safety—the cliché is right—begins at
home. At least, that is one place where you have
control over it. Before you bring home a small, in-
quisitive kitten or a large, curious cat, a safety check
is a necessity. Houseplants have been mentioned before; there are lists of these and other potential house-

hold poisons in more comprehensive cat-care books. Plastic bags are just as fascinating to cats as paper bags, but they can be lethal. Hiding places like closets, drawers, even ovens and clothes dryers are problems you must keep in the back of your mind from now on. Dangling electric cords are temptations, as are rubber bands, string, and open windows without screens. Just as you would take obstacles and temptations out of the route of a small child, so you must with your cat, particularly at the beginning. All cats are curious, but not all of them are cautious, and none of them really has nine lives.

Preventative medicine catches problems before they become panics. If you watch your cat's diet, observe his daily behavior with an eye to changes in appearance or attitude, and help with the once-a-week grooming, you are on your way to doing just that. Along with the grooming, you can also check for fleas and other unwelcome guests, watch for any swellings or sore spots, and check for ear mites.

On the ticklish subject of fleas, many vets recommend a flea collar, loosely fastened around the cat's neck. A dusting with flea powder is a good idea, too. Read the instructions on all de-flea preparations first, and keep an eye out for any allergic reactions such as thinning fur or small, irritated spots. If the cat is infested with fleas, of course, bathe with a medicated cat shampoo; air, vacuum, and heavily powder the cat's bed; and get that collar. Ear mites and their compatriots, head and harvest mites, are a removal job for the vet, as are worms. For diagnosis of the latter, the vet will need a fecal sample, so take one with you to checkups to avoid extra trips.

If the cat's eyes seem irritated, there may be a speck or some small irritant present. Using an eyedropper with a boric acid solution (1 teaspoon boric acid to 1 pint water), wash the eye. If the condition persists or if the third eyelid, that strange, filmy contraption that comes out from the nose side to cover the cat's eye, is frequently seen, ask your vet for further instructions. Some cats do use the third eyelid simply as a light barrier when napping.

Cats also catch colds, which make them sneeze and their noses run. This may mean only that the cat should stay indoors and keep warm until it is over. Often keeping the cat in a room with a vaporizer makes recovery quicker. Any cold that lasts more than a few days, however, or is accompanied by coughing, is probably more serious and deserves professional attention. Coughing is neither normal nor easy behavior for a cat and is a signal of possible problems.

Vomiting is usually for one of two reasons: one, because the cat is genuinely ill, or two, because the cat has eaten something it wishes it hadn't, the latter being more frequent and occurring soon after eating. The answer is usually simple: either the food was the wrong temperature, had been out for too long or contained some ingredient that upset the cat, or the cat ate too much or too fast. When vomiting occurs, watch the cat for signs of unusual behavior or prolonged dry retching. At the end of twelve hours, feed the cat a small meal of bland food—baby food, cottage cheese, soft-cooked egg. If that stays down, try a little more of the same, and by the next day, all will probably be back to normal.

Hairballs, another cause of vomiting, can be prevented by feeding the cat small amounts of petroleum jelly. There are flavored versions that come in tubes, purchasable at your local pet store. Most cats consider these candy. Mineral oil can also be added to the cat's food at the rate of one teaspoon per ten pounds of cat. This also aids in discouraging elimination problems.

Diarrhea is usually a sign of dietary problems. Many times it is triggered by milk. This is an easy one to spot. Cut out the milk and see if the problem stops. Psychological stress, a trip to the vet in a car, for example, or some particular pet food formula may also cause diarrhea. The treatment is simple: a twelve- to twenty-four-hour fast followed by a bland diet such as baby food, soft-cooked eggs, or chicken. If diarrhea persists longer than twenty-four to thirty-six hours, head for the vet with fecal samples.

Anything to do with the genitourinary system belongs at the vet. Home remedies and self-healing do not apply.

A cat's vital signs are the same as a human's: temperature, pulse, rate of respiration. The cat's temperature at rest is between 101.0 and 102.5 degrees F. The temperature must be taken rectally, which is no job for a novice. The pulse is 110 to 130 beats per minute and can be taken at the femoral artery on the inner side of the hip joint of the hind leg. Normal rate of respiration is twenty to thirty breaths per minute. Any change in any of these signals is a problem.

Know your cat. Handle your cat. Know when bumps develop. PAY ATTENTION. There are signs of trouble long before things get serious.

94

On hand in some predetermined place you should keep a feline first aid kit. It should contain the following items:

> Bandages (or clean cloth for making them)
> Sterile gauze pads
> Adhesive tape
> Petroleum jelly and/or mineral oil
> Hydrogen peroxide
> Sterile cotton and/or cotton-tipped swabs
> Blunt-nosed tweezers
> Eyedropper
> Teaspoon (measuring and administering doses)
> Antiseptic powder, spray, or medication
> Tranquilizers, antibiotics, etc., at the prescription of your vet,
>   labeled with date, dosage, and indications

In addition to the above, the name, address, phone numbers, and business hours of your veterinarian should be in the kit. If you don't write these down, especially the latter, you will be unable to remember them in an emergency. It is almost axiomatic. Another excellent addition to the complete kit is the *Angell Memorial Guide to Animal First Aid*. Inexpensive, clear, and useable, this pamphlet is listed in the Appendix along with information on how to obtain it. It should have a ten-star rating in anyone's system.

Prompt and knowledgeable action in emergency situations increases chances of recovery immeasurably, as well as giving the owner an antidote for that panicky, helpless feeling that usually follows being faced with an ill or injured animal. Here, then, is a quick guide through what to look for, what probably happened, and how to help your cat through some of the more common medical problems.

BITES, CUTS, AND OTHER COMBAT WOUNDS. A fresh wound responds easily to home first aid. Shallow cuts, tears, and scratches should be washed clean with hydrogen peroxide. The foaming action lifts out particles, and application should be continued until foaming stops. Unless the wound is in an unreachable spot, an animal can heal it itself after the initial cleansing. Most cuts will stop bleeding within five to six minutes. If bleeding does not stop, clean the wound again, place a gauze pad or any clean cloth over the wound, and then wrap it firmly but not tightly with more gauze, clean strips of cloth, or an elastic bandage. If this works, you can wait to see the vet. However, if the wound is big or deep, don't figure it will heal itself. Antibiotics are in order. Tourniquets are a last-ditch resort if bleeding is copious and will not stop. They are useful only on limbs or tail and must be loosened every fifteen minutes. Once the bleeding is under control, put on a pressure bandage as described above and go immediately to your vet.

ABSCESSES. Abscesses develop from wounds that are unnoticed and/or too deep to clean thoroughly. If you find a sensitive lump, which is usually hot to the touch and which your cat quite evidently wants you to leave alone, you have probably come upon an old wound that has become infected. If it has broken and is draining, clean it with a cotton swab or gauze pad dipped in three percent hydrogen peroxide or pour the solution directly on it or, in the case of a deep hole, use an eyedropper to get pressure. Clean the wound several times and keep an eye on it. If, however, the whole area seems hot and/or the lump is not open and the cat has a fever or other signs of illness, do not attempt home treatment without consultation.

FRACTURES, DISLOCATIONS, AND SPRAINS. These are usually caused by car accidents but may be a result of a fight with a larger animal. If the animal will lie quietly and there will be little delay in reaching a vet, do not bother with a splint. If one is needed, a straight, rigid object such as a stick or even a tightly rolled newspaper will do to hold the limb rigid. Do not tie the area of the break to the splint, and pad the splint as much as possible. It is almost impossible for a layman to tell the difference between a fracture (unless the bone is sticking out), a sprain, or a dislocation. Don't waste time trying.

BURNS, ELECTRICAL AND OTHERWISE. For thermal burns from hot liquids or direct fire or heat, apply cold water or ice compresses to the affected area for twenty minutes. Then put on antiburn ointment or soak the area with a sterile pad dipped in strong tea. Cover with petroleum jelly. For acid or alkali burns, immediately flush the skin with lots of water. For electrical burns, often caused by chewing on electrical cords, warm the animal in a towel or blanket and keep it warm. Watch for signs of shock such as low vital signs, dazed appearance, or rapid, shallow breathing, which may show up many hours later.

FOREIGN OBJECTS IN MOUTH OR THROAT. The cat will usually clue you in to this one by pawing at its mouth or moving it in a strange way. If you work gently, you can usually find the object, which might be string, small pieces of bone, or a splinter. Remove all except the first with your fingers or tweezers. Swallowing string or thread is a common problem and can be quite dangerous; the same goes for yarn, all of which may get entangled in the intestines and cause an internal blockage. If you see a thread hanging out of either end of your cat, don't just pull, either. There may just be a needle on the other end, and who knows which way it lies? It's happened.

HEATSTROKE. This condition is easily avoided by following one simple rule: never leave a cat in a car or any other small, enclosed place in hot weather. If heatstroke should occur, get the cat to a cool place immediately and keep the fur damp with cool water. When the cat stirs, feed it a spoonful of strong coffee. Give water in small amounts.

POISON, INDOORS AND OUTDOORS. Poison may be inhaled, swallowed, or absorbed through the skin. There are extensive poison charts in the Angell Memorial first aid pamphlet and in all the cat-care books I have recommended. These charts reveal things that would amaze you, such as antifreeze, which cats love; human medications such as aspirin and iodine; and road salt. Wash your cat's feet in the winter. It may sound silly, but if you don't, the cat will, and road salt is toxic. There are also, as mentioned in the previous chapter, plants that are detrimental to feline health. Each poisoning has its own symptoms and antidote, some of which are pretty esoteric. The antidote for antifreeze, for example, is vodka and milk.

Important considerations under first aid are special bandages for special occasions and procedures such as restraints. An example of a special bandage that keeps the cat from scratching a head injury is the so-called Elizabethan collar, a circular plastic or cardboard collar that takes its name from its resemblance to the Elizabethan ruff. A light bandage for an injured foot can be made from a doll or baby sock loosely taped to the leg. Restraint can be as simple as a towel wrapped around the cat or as tough as the classic pillowcase or old trouser leg.

Unlike dogs, cats do not sit on command while visiting the vet or going through procedures not to their liking. For light physical restraint, wrap one arm around the cat's body so that the head is restricted between the arm and the body and your hand is firmly on the cat's rear legs. This hold takes a little practice. Holding the cat by the scruff of the neck with the arm extended down the cat's back is another solid hold, leaving you with a free hand.

Home nursing is mostly common sense plus knowing your cat. There are a few small things to remember. When a cat is sick, it dislikes being messy. Gentle grooming and cleaning make things more pleasant all around, but don't fuss. Keep eyes, ears, and nose clean. If the cat has diarrhea, clean it gently and use petroleum jelly or a nonperfumed cold cream to treat soreness. Don't worry if a cat with a cold doesn't eat much; cats don't like to eat food they cannot smell.

The birth of kittens is something else, a natural process in which the owner is simply on standby in case of problems. If you are sensible, you will stand by with a cat-care book in hand, with all sections dealing with potential problems well marked and with your vet's number on the phone stand. That way nobody will have any problems, and you will all feel very smug. Like the taxi driver who finds that he must function as a midwife, you will probably feel quite helpless and out of place. Don't worry; the mother cat will probably take care of everything with nothing except cheers from you.

A few facts on what to expect are helpful. Gestation takes fifty-six to sixty-five days, sixty-three is average. Incidentally, seventy-one is the longest on record; if gestation goes longer than that, you probably have either a false pregnancy or a real problem. Delivery usually takes two to six hours, depending on the number of kittens, the average litter being three to five. The mother cat will usually rest for ten to fifteen minutes between kittens. For further details, ask your vet or read one of the recommended books.

Keep cat and kittens indoors and leave them pretty much alone for the first little while. Handle as little as possible. The kittens will, at first, be quiet and do a lot of sleeping and eating. The umbilical cords will fall off two to three days after birth, and eyes will open in ten to twelve days. By five weeks, the kittens will have their baby teeth. At three to four weeks, however, they can begin to shift to small amounts of dilute, high-protein pablum, meat or egg-yolk baby food and can learn to lap milk from a saucer. By five weeks, they should be on solid food. All changes in feeding should be made gradually so as to avoid digestive upsets.

Incidentally, pregnant and lactating cats need extra protein but not extra amounts of food. This is true especially toward the end of a pregnancy when mothers-to-be would rather eat several small meals than one large meal a day.

Cats, like humans, are living longer, and the care of the geriatric feline has become a part of veterinary practice. There are special diets, new medications, and a lot more information on the subject. Growing old gracefully is not or should not be restricted to humans.

Now we come to a person who has been mentioned many times in these last two chapters, your veterinarian. This is no p.r. job for vets; there are good ones and bad ones, as with any profession, and a great deal of your feeling for your vet will be based on personal observations. The point is that the animal's body is the veterinarian's job; and the more complex the problem, the less likely the average pet owner is to be able to cope with it. Do not expect your vet to be James Herriot any more than you would expect your personal physician to be Marcus Welby, M.D. Here are a few things to look for when you make your first visit.

First and foremost, unless this is the only veterinary practice in town, ask around and weigh your friends' opinions of their vets. The most important thing in my opinion is the way the vet handles the cat. This is probably a personal bias, but I have moved about enough to feel that any animal knows, particularly in times of stress and panic (which describe any visit to the vet for most cats), the feel of safety in sure hands. The office and the waiting room should be clean, of course, and appointments and records managed efficiently. Also important are the attitude and thoroughness of the vet in answering your questions and the kind of answers you get.

It is a good idea to take your new kitten to your vet right after you get it, even if the breeder has made sure the kitten shots were given. The first vaccination is given at eight to ten weeks of age and is for cat distemper, which is a viral killer, particularly of young cats. The disease shows few signs until it is established and the cat has little chance of recovery. At this time, the vet will give the kitten a thorough physical. It is a good idea to bring a fecal sample, as I have mentioned before, to avoid an extra trip. There is usually a second distemper shot two weeks later.

At this time, make a permanent record of all shots, illnesses, and problems your cat encounters. It is a memory jogger and should be included with the information on your vet's hours and phone numbers in your first aid kit and/or with your copy of your cat's registration papers.

Rabies shots were once considered unnecessary for cats. They still are for totally indoor cats; but suburban and country cats should have their shots, the first at three to four months, and then a booster at one- to two-year intervals.

These are a few rough ideas of the problems you may encounter. My advice is threefold:

1) Get a detailed book on cat care and read it through at least once so that you are familiar with its contents.

2) Make up a first aid kit, complete with records, which is always in the same handy place.

3) Find a vet you and your cat trust, one who likes animals and doesn't mind questions. Keep the vet's card and a list of his or her hours in the first aid kit and, if you're like me, another set in your book on cat care and a third in your phone book.

Then, with a little bit of luck, you will all live happily ever after.

Epilogue

Throughout this book, with the exception of the last two general chapters, I have been giving the history of a breed of which I am exceedingly proud and fond, but with a light touch.

Do I seem to be laughing at these cats, not to be taking them seriously? Wrong. The chuckle is one of sheer delight. For here is a cat with a dry sense of humor and perspective, one that seems to take its newfound position in the limelight with a big grain of sea salt, an attitude people would do well to emulate. Here is a cat of substance and background, a breed that has seen good times and bad and handled both quite capably. This cat is neither stolid nor stylish, highbrow nor high-strung. Man didn't form it in the first place, and, with any luck, man won't ruin it either.

Let there be no mistake. I applaud the dedicated breeders, I cheer the devoted fanciers, but first and foremost, I champion the healthy, companionable cat.

For as a famous cat lover, Mark Twain, so aptly put it, "If the cat were crossed with man, it would be very good for man, but ruinacious for the cat."

How goes it with you, cat?

I hope, over the years to come, we can all answer, "Well."

Appendix

FOR MORE INFORMATION ON THE CAT (AND HIS RELATIVES):
The Complete Guide to Cats by James Richards, DVM, Chronicle
Books.

FOR MORE INFORMATION ON BREEDING AND SHOWING:
*Caring For, Breeding, and Showing Your Maine Coon Cat: A Guide to
Cattery Management*, edited by Michael and Patricia Simpson, Maine
Coon Breeders and Fanciers Association, 1991. To order send $7 to
13283 Deron Ave., San Diego, CA 92129.

FOR ALL-PURPOSE FIRST AID, PREVENTATIVE CARE, AND NUTRITION
INFORMATION:
The Veterinarian's Guide to Natural Remedies for Cats by Martin Zucker,
Three Rivers Press.
Cat First Aid by Charles Boyle, Storey Publications.
Catwatch (newsletter), Cornell University College of Veterinary
Medicine, PO Box 420234, Palm Coast, FL 32142-0234.
Catnip (newsletter), Tufts University School of Veterinary Medicine,
PO Box 420070, Palm Coast, FL 32142-9571.

FOR INFORMATION ON THE BREED AND ITS FUTURE:
Maine Coon Breeders and Fanciers (all names and addresses as of
2002): President: Vicki Shipp, 2719 Wicklow Drive, Augusta, GA
30909; Corresponding Secretary (and source of information on books,
pamphlets, etc.): Deborah Hall, 4405 Karroll SW, Albuquerque, NM
87121; *The Scratch Sheet* Editor: Kit Mounger, 485 Cottontail Lane,
Afton, TN 37616.

FOR THE COMPUTER LITERATE:
Maine Coon Breeders and Fanciers Association www.mcbfa.org
Maine Coon Breeders www.breedlist.com/maine-coon-breeders.html
Maine Coon Alliance www.mainecoonalliance.org
Maine Coon Cat Club (UK) www.maine-coon-cat-club.com
Absolutely Cats: Maine Coon Breeders (international):
http://members.tripod.com/~kcwingwalker/23MaineCoon.html
Maine Coon database www.tdb.uu.se/cgi-bin/MCO
Maine Coon chat room mcats@yahoogroups.com
Cat Fanciers, breed facts www.fanciers.combreed-faqs/maine-coon-
faw/html
Cat Fanciers, breed profile www.cfainc.org/breeds/profiles/maine.html
Registration association websites: www.cfainc.org   www.cffinc.org
www.ccfacat.com   www.tica.org